Protection
Magick

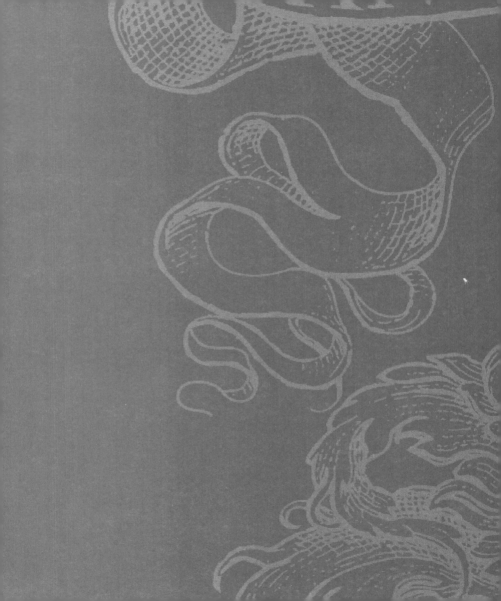

Protection Magick

Spells for Defense

CASSANDRA EASON

AUTHOR OF *1001 SPELLS*

STERLING ETHOS
New York

STERLING ETHOS
New York

An Imprint of Sterling Publishing Co., Inc.
1166 Avenue of the Americas
New York, NY 10036

ISBN 978-1-4549-3350-2

Distributed in Canada by Sterling Publishing Co., Inc.
^{c}/o Canadian Manda Group, 664 Annette Street
Toronto, Ontario M6S 2C8, Canada
Distributed in the United Kingdom by GMC Distribution Services
Castle Place, 166 High Street, Lewes, East Sussex BN7 1XU, England
Distributed in Australia by NewSouth Books
University of New South Wales, Sydney, NSW 2052, Australia

For information about custom editions,
special sales, and premium and corporate purchases,
please contact Sterling Special Sales at 800-805-5489
or specialsales@sterlingpublishing.com.

Manufactured in China

2 4 6 8 10 9 7 5 3 1

sterlingpublishing.com

Cover design by Elizabeth Mihaltse Lindy
Interior design by Christine Heun, with Sharon Jacobs

Image Credits: iStock (throughout): PeterHermesFurian; imaginasty; olgagriga;
vectortatu; lllerlok_Xolms; SharonJacobs (throughout); Shutterstock: (cover, throughout)
Angie Makes; ararat.art; MysticalLink; Hein Nouwens; Pinchuk Oleksandra

Images on cover and throughout interior from Getty/iStock
Sigil art (cover) created using Sigilscribe (sigilscribe.me) by Metatronix

DEDICATION

To my beloved family, Jade, Miranda, Tom, Jack,
Bill, Freya, Holly and Oliver, with special thanks to
Kate Zimmermann, Konnie, and John Gold,
who have all inspired and guided me.

Contents

Introduction

Protective or shielding magick has three phases: first, the removal of malice and negativity if a physical, psychological, or psychic attack has occurred or is threatened. Second, protection from future attack and its effects. And the third all-important and positive aspect is the restoration of good fortune, success, health, or harmony. Without the third phase, there is a vacuum that can be filled by low life energies if left empty, so the key to successful shielding magick is always to replace what you have banished. Therefore, the spells in this book are empowering as well as protective.

The spells, one a day for a year, cover every aspect of protection against traditional forms of ill-wishing:

* *Curses made consciously or unconsciously against individuals, families, homes, or businesses*

* *Jinxes that bring on ill fortune to prevent a person from succeeding*

* *Hexes, which are formal and often specific curses deliberately cast by a magical practitioner, usually in return for money (or by an irresponsible amateur playing occult power games)*

* *The evil eye of envy (more on this in Chapter 8)*

But this book also focuses on repelling everyday nastiness from those with whom we come into contact in our daily lives. This includes bullying on social media, protection from an obsessive or violent ex-partner, protection from financial fraud, from ill health, from infertility, from vandalism, from becoming a victim of terrorism, from paranormal and psychic attack, and from fears and phobias that may hold us back from happiness. Because, most of all, we need shielding from everyday dangers and crises, the spells are quick, easy to cast, use everyday materials, and the majority are related to the hazards of the world in which we live and work.

What You Need for Shielding Spells

Each protective spell in the book contains a list of what you will need, most of which you already will have in your cupboard or toolbox, or items that can easily be obtained from the local supermarket, garden center, or home improvement store. There is no need to buy specialty magical equipment, though you might if you practice magick regularly and want to collect one or two beautiful items you may find in an antiques store. Many of the spell items are in everyday use. Candle snuffers, for example, are common in stores that sell candles, but you can easily use metal tongs to snuff out a candle and so extinguish the power of a bully.

I have suggested different candle colors and fragrances as most appropriate. However, you can substitute an all-purpose white candle or a generic fragrance, such as rose, lavender, or sandalwood. Incense sticks and cones are ideal for casting spells in a hurry. Potpourri is an excellent substitute for petals, although you can pluck the petals from a fresh rose or another flower of the suggested color. Most of the herbs you need in magick can be found in the culinary section of the local supermarket, or try your local health food store for less common plants, such as dried nettles, that are ideal for a fiercely defensive charm bag. You can empower herbs in a spell and afterwards use them in cooking for ongoing protection.

You may wish to keep a well-stocked box with different-colored candles, incense sticks, candleholders, etc. if you cast a lot of spells, but otherwise raid your household supplies before spell-casting. Candles used in the later stages of a spell to restore light, health, and fortune, or to offer protection, can be burned around the home in the days after the spell, though those used for banishing or binding should be environmentally disposed of after the spell. Household appliances, such as a freezer, are your best friend for binding the names of those doing or wishing harm written on paper in the coldest part of the freezer. You will need soil or sand to bury burned cords (a big planter is ideal if you live in an apartment).

Have a sharp knife handy (one with a silver-colored handle is best) and scissors for symbolically cutting destructive links, plus strong sewing thread, string, curtain cords, or ribbons in different colors for knot-tying and binding malice.

Look in advance for places near where you will customarily cast spells to bury small items after a spell. Also, find a source of nearby running water to cast petals or seeds (if necessary, use a bucket or bowl of water and pour it into the ground) and where you can scatter seeds or petals into the air (even from an upstairs window). For fire, think barbecue coals, bonfires, or candles set in a large heatproof base so you can safely burn threads and scatter salt or herbs in the flame.

Pick up a current calendar listing dates with daily moon phases and the zodiac signs through which the moon passes each month, or access a good online site, for example, https://www.moongiant.com/fullmoons, which gives you the universal moon times so you can work out the moon phases in your own location, or http://starsignstyle.com/full-moon-calendar, which contains the zodiac signs of the different full moons.

The moon is a very powerful energy in all its phases, though different days of the week and times of the day are also important. But if a need is urgent, you can cast a spell at any time and then repeat it at the suggested time. Timings are ideal but not mandatory.

How to Cast Spells

You will need a space, a table, or any flat surface, indoors or out, on which to place all your ingredients before starting a spell. However, there is no need to keep this just for magick. If you want to create an altar, for informal spells, the home, hearth, and garden have for thousands of years been the site and source where magick has been carried out by ordinary people and community wise women and men for daily needs.

Look in the appropriate section of the book for the right spell, using the index to narrow down your choices.

Protection While Spell Casting

While in formal or ritual magick, there can be quite elaborate preparations, such as casting a circle and closing ceremonies, the spells in this book are informal and cast for a specific purpose, rather than as part of a magical celebration or offerings ceremony.

But the spells in this and, indeed, my other Sterling Ethos spell books follow the tradition of folk magick, only to deflect harm from the innocent, carried out with good intention to harm no one. Therefore, these spells contain built-in protection.

However, before beginning, you can, if you wish, hold a pointed crystal quartz or a clear quartz crystal massage wand in your dominant hand or use the index finger of your dominant hand with the second finger joined to it horizontally outward or the whole hand, fingers together and pointing outward and facing the area where you will be casting your spell.

Hold the crystal outward, straight ahead, and visualize drawing around you clockwise and including in the spell area a circle of shimmering light from the ground, rising up like walls of light, extending above the whole space like a shimmering star (include yourself within the light), then fading but present throughout the spell. Ask silently, *May only goodness and light enter here.*

When you finish the spell, reverse the process and if you used a pointed crystal, wash it under running water. Alternatively, picture directly ahead of you as you face the spell table or the outdoor space in which you will be working, Uriel, archangel of the earth, in indigo robes with his torch of fire, then, to your right-hand side, Raphael, archangel of healing, in his robes of early morning sunlight, and behind you the glorious red and gold Michael, archangel of the sun, and to your left the starry Gabriel, archangel of the moon. Ask the four archangels to cast their shimmering light all around you and the spell area and picture this brilliance extending as a star of light over your head and including the spell table or outdoor space. Afterwards, thank the archangels and the light will fade to be reactivated whenever you call upon them.

Using the Right Words and Format

Read the spell two or three times before beginning, and feel free to change words or actions that don't feel right. Write down any key words you will be using and, if you wish, you can read the words during the spell. Memorize the order of the spell and have a run-through of the spell actions and words before starting, to check that you have everything you need within reach. If possible, make sure you will be undisturbed during the spell, unless someone is sharing the spell with you. Switch off all mobile devices or put them on silent and, unless it

is a spell involving technological equipment, try to have these out of the room or cover them.

However, if you are sharing a crowded apartment or are dealing with the constant demands of small children, you can cast any of the spells in this book simply by reading them slowly at the appropriate time and visualizing them. (I used to improvise spells on the seashore while the children were building sandcastles and made many a circle and labyrinth in the sand.) Each spell is empowered by its creation and can be activated by the simple act of reading. Perhaps light a candle or hold an object you are going to endow as a protective charm as you read. With practice, it is possible to cast a spell entirely in your mind while working, driving a child to kindergarten, or in a noisy office.

If you can memorize the words and say them in your mind, so much the better.

Magical power can be stored in a spell through using a sigil or magical symbol. In this book, I have suggested symbols that belong to ancient cultures such as the hieroglyphs of Old Egypt or the runes of the Norse world. These contain within them the actual power of the meaning of the symbol that is released by the spell. You can, if, for example, you want to empower a protective amulet for a hostile workplace, draw the symbol in incense smoke in the air over a piece of jewelry you often wear. You can also draw invisible symbols over items you use daily, such as car keys or a memory stick, and trace protective pentagrams that I describe in spells in the book in water over doors and windows to keep away thieves.

Remember, if any part of any spell does not feel right, adapt it to suit your needs, for all the spells are templates and, like any template, can be made to fit your needs. You cannot make mistakes magically if you work with a good heart and pure intention, and no one is sitting in the sky ensuring you say every word as specified or move counter instead of clockwise. Enjoy spellcasting.

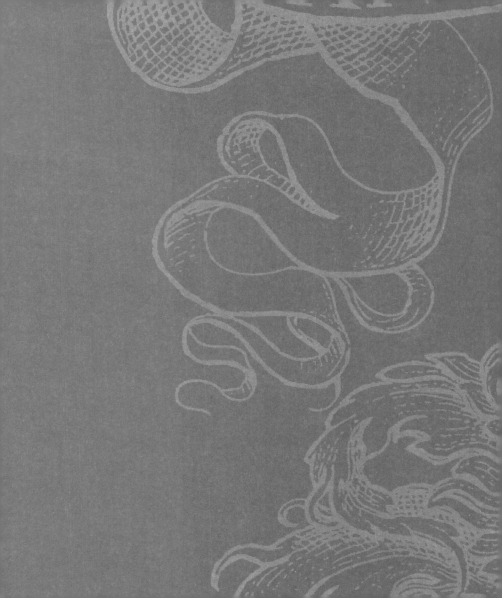

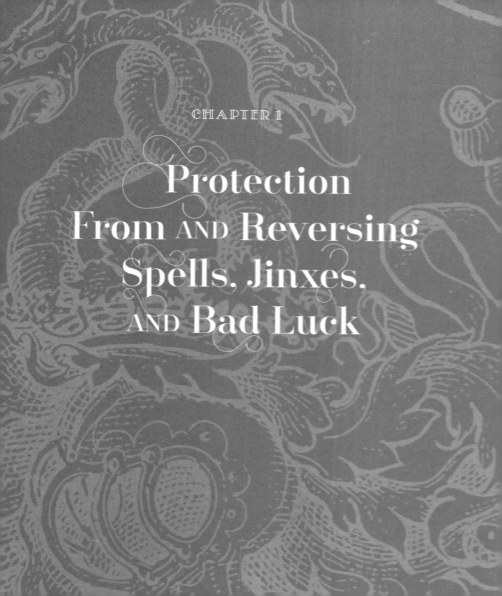

CHAPTER 1

Protection From AND Reversing Spells, Jinxes, AND Bad Luck

A jinx is defined as the attraction of bad fortune for a specific event or situation that prevents the person or event from succeeding. Sometimes it is believed that we jinx ourselves by being overconfident. When we're jinxed by others, unlike the evil eye, it is not caused by envy but by deliberate ill-wishing specifically to prevent our success.

Bad luck itself is like a psychic snowball. Once things start going wrong, we become jittery, lose focus, and bad luck accumulates psychically and psychologically. Bad luck can be caused initially by random cosmic events; some believe by the position of our stars or by someone wishing us ill fortune. The following spells will block and reverse misfortune and bring good luck no matter what the original cause of the misfortune.

Reversing Bad Luck

YOU WILL NEED

A purple candle ✷ A white candle
✷ A piece of long, strong purple thread ✷ A candle snuffer
✷ A piece of long, strong white thread

TIMING

Thursday, the day of Barakiel, archangel of good fortune.

THE SPELL

* Place the purple candle to the left of the white one.

* Invisibly trace with your index finger on the unlit purple candle,
  BAD LUCK BANISHED BE and on the white one GOOD LUCK COME TO ME.

* Light the purple candle, saying, *Misfortune, there is the door.*
  Trouble me no more.

* Light the white candle from the purple one, saying, *Good luck waiting*
  in the wings that joy brings.

* Tie a knot in the purple thread, saying, *Misfortune be bound,*
  no more found.

* Extinguish the purple candle with the snuffer, saying, *Bad luck,*
  dark luck, gone your power, done.

* Blow out the white candle, saying, *Lucky and luckier shall I be.*

* Hang the purple knotted thread outdoors, saying, *Bad luck enter*
  here no more, I shut the door.

* Hang the unknotted white cord above the front door, just inside.

If You are Unlucky in Love

YOU WILL NEED

A silver heart on a knotted pink ribbon ★ A sharp knife or
scissors ★ An envelope ★ A red pen ★ A long silver chain

TIMING

Monday, the day of Geliel, angel who restores luck in love

THE SPELL

∗ Hold the ribbon, saying, *Break now the ties of love untrue.*
No more shall I suffer you.

∗ Unknot the ribbon and release the heart from the ribbon, saying,
Misfortune in love here we part. I go to find that loving heart.

∗ Cut the ribbon into small pieces and seal them in the envelope,
writing on the front, NO LONGER WANTED.

∗ Put the heart on the silver chain and wear it whenever you go
out socially, saying, *Good fortune in love and a new start,*
I go to find that loving heart.

∗ Place the envelope in a garbage bin far away from your house.

If You are Unlucky in Money

YOU WILL NEED

A green candle ✶ Three Chinese divinatory coins
(or any gold-colored coins) ✶ A green bag
or purse (the color of good fortune)

TIMING

Early morning

THE SPELL

* Invisibly trace dollars or local currency signs all over the unlit candle with your little (money) finger.

* Light the candle and toss the coins in your open-cupped hands, saying, *Lucky, lucky, lucky in money shall I be, bad luck no more financially for me.*

* Toss the coins higher and chant faster until you can move and speak no faster, then slow down and catch the coins, slowly and quietly saying the spell words once more.

* Put the coins in the bag and close it, saying three times, *My financial luck has changed. Good fortune permanently is arranged.*

* Blow out the candle and keep the bag with you during financial dealings.

To Reverse a Jinx if You Have Attracted Bad Luck by Someone's Ill-Wishing

A thin strip of paper ★ A soluble blue ink marker pen
★ A small, deep bowl of water

TIMING

Evening before sunset

THE SPELL

* Say, *Jinx, jinx, jinx, three by three, unjinxed now must I be.*
  My success cannot you blockade, your dissolution I have made.

* On the paper, copy these spell words with the soluble blue ink from
  the end of the strip to the beginning: MADE HAVE I DISSOLUTION YOUR,
  BLOCKADE YOU CANNOT SUCCESS MY, BE I MUST NOW UNJINXED,
  THREE BY THREE, JINX, JINX JINX.

* Soak the paper in the water until the ink dissolves or blurs the words
  and the paper starts to disintegrate.

* Pour the contents into a hole where no plants grow, or in a waterproof
  garbage can, and wash out the bowl.

To Avoid Jinxing Yourself Before Competing or Going for What You Want

Dried or powdered nettles from a health food store
or online ★ Two small bowls ★ Garlic salt
or granules ★ Two paper bags

TIMING

As darkness falls

THE SPELL

* Pour a small quantity of nettles into the first bowl and hold the bowl for a minute or two, but do not mix the nettles. Say, *Jinx, jinx, jinx. Unwanted minx, I will not jinx myself, with your tricks. Your ingredients I shall not mix, your unlucky recipe I will not fix.*

* Now add some garlic granules to the second bowl and again hold the bowl but do not mix it.

* Add the nettles to one bag and the garlic to the other, making sure they do not touch, and seal them firmly.

* Put them in separate garbage bins away from your home.

If You are always Breaking Precious Items or Equipment at Home or Work

YOU WILL NEED

A delicate precious item from within the home
★ A large feather

TIMING

Saturday, the day of caution

THE SPELL

* Stand in front of, but not too, near the precious item.

* Gently waft the feather in front of it, but not too close, saying softly and rhythmically, *Cautiously, gently, softly, do not shatter, do not break. Do not splinter or cease to work under my touch, I ask this much.*

* Continue to walk around the home with the feather in front of anything valuable and fragile, repeating the spell words and actions.

* If office equipment ceases to function the minute you touch it, before using it gently and surreptitiously, move your dominant hand vertically nine times in front of it and say the spell words nine times in your mind, then approach it slowly and calmly.

A Charm Bag to Keep
Misfortune from Your Life

YOU WILL NEED

Five of the following: allspice, basil, chamomile, dill, juniper berries,
lavender, lemon balm (Melissa), rosemary, thyme, or vetivert
★ A bowl and a spoon ★ A green drawstring bag or purse
★ Five golden-colored coins or green currency notes ★ Salt
★ Five hairs from your head ★ Patchouli or sandalwood oil

TIMING

The day before the crescent moon

THE SPELL

* Add the herbs one by one to the bowl, mixing with the spoon after each
  addition, first counterclockwise, then clockwise, five times each way,
  saying, *Five by five, the spell's alive. Bad fortune shall no longer be.
  Only good luck may come to me.*

* Place the herbs in the bag. Add the coins, five pinches of salt, and the hairs,
  blending with a few drops of oil saying, *Five by five, in vain bad fortune
  strive. This bag shall be, guardian of good luck, health, and prosperity.*

* Close the bag, hiding it where it will not be discovered. Replace
  the contents when the bag loses its fragrance and use the bag until
  good luck shines on the person casting the spell.

To Change Bad Luck into Good,
Using the Waning and Crescent Moon

YOU WILL NEED

A glass bowl of water ★ White or apple cider
vinegar ★ Dried rosemary thyme, sage, and mint

TIMING

After dark, at the end of the waning moon cycle

THE SPELL

* Take the bowl outdoors. To the water add nine drops of vinegar and a handful of herbs.

* Swirl the bowl in both directions alternately, saying, *Bad luck, I give you to Grandmother Moon, to take away all sorrow and bring better tomorrows, very soon.*

* Dip your index finger in the water and lick it, saying, *Grandmother, I take in your power, to transform misfortune at this hour.*

* Leave the bowl in a sheltered place and, once you see the crescent moon in the sky, pour the water onto the ground, saying, *All misfortune I pour away, rising moon, bring good luck to stay.*

To Break a Specific Run
of Bad Luck in Your Life

YOU WILL NEED

Make a calendar with a numbered square for each day of
the current year up to the present day marked in pencil,
starting with the time the ill luck began ✳ An eraser
✳ A sharp scissors ✳ A new store-bought calendar

TIMING

The end of a week

THE SPELL

✳ Go from the present day backwards and erase each square number,
saying, *Misfortune I erase, unlucky nights and days. Unwritten as though
they never had been, no longer in my life shall bad luck be seen.*

✳ When the squares are empty, cut up the squares from the present day
to the beginning of the year, saying, *Cut up, banished, disappeared,
ahead lie fortunate days, months, and lucky years.*

✳ Burn the cut-up squares and hang the new calendar on the wall,
marking the present day, as *the best day ever.*

To Avert Bad Luck if You Have Broken a Lucky Talisman or a Mirror, Which Traditionally Brings Seven Years of Bad Luck

YOU WILL NEED

The broken pieces * A strong dark piece of cloth * Dried tarragon, the protective dragon's herb * A piece of dark-colored string * A soft white cloth

TIMING

After the breakage

THE SPELL

* Set the broken pieces on the dark cloth and sprinkle tarragon on top, saying, *Seven years of bad luck are not to be, misfortune come not after me.*

* Wrap the broken pieces securely in the dark-colored cloth and tie it with four knots of the dark-colored string, one on top of the other, saying, *Four square, locked and bound around, no trace in my life of bad luck shall be found.*

* Put the parcel on a high, dark shelf for seven years.

* Buy a new mirror or an identical talisman, and polish it with a soft white cloth, saying, *Light enter this mirror/charm and shine. Henceforward, good fortune shall be mine.*

To Start Again if You Have Been Unlucky for Most of Your Life

Peppercorns ⋆ Rosemary ⋆ Sage ⋆ Dried cloves ⋆ A small jug of apple cider vinegar ⋆ A larger jug of water in which rose petals have been soaked for a few hours

TIMING

The end of a day, week, or month

THE SPELL

* Add the peppercorns, rosemary, sage, and cloves to the jug with the vinegar and swirl the jug three times each way, saying, *Bad luck too long has lingered in my life, obstructing my path and causing me strife.*

* Go out of your front door and pour the vinegar in a thin line, right to left, ahead of you as you stand close to and facing away from the door.

* Now, standing even closer to the front door, ahead of you, left to right, pour the rose water in a line, saying, *New life, new fortune begins from here. Good luck is mine, I have drawn the line.*

13

If You Lose a Lucky Charm and Fear the End of Good Fortune

YOU WILL NEED

A replacement of the lost charm, as closely resembling the lost item
as possible ★ A small sealable cloth bag ★ A sealable bag of salt

TIMING

The new moon before it becomes visible in the sky

THE SPELL

* Hold the replacement item between your open-cupped hands, close
  your hands over it and say, *I impress you, no less, with accumulated
  good fortune, I have gained in the past, and this time will last.
  Good luck passes through me to you, as the new moon grows it shall be so,
  and good luck regrow.*

* Wrap the charm in the cloth bag, enclose that bag in the bag of salt,
  and bury it, marking the place. Dig it up when the crescent moon can
  be seen in the sky.

* Throw away the bag of salt and carry your new charm with confidence.

To Avert Bad Luck if Your Personal Astrological Chart is Against You or Mercury is in Retrograde

Note: People would already know the stars were unlucky or they would not be doing this spell in the first place.

YOU WILL NEED

A long strip of paper on which is written in red ink, I SHALL BE LUCKY WHATEVER THE STARS SAY. (You can check your stars or Mercury position online or in the astrological section of any daily journal) ✳ A clear glass jar or a bottle with a lid ✳ A pile of precut short red threads ✳ A chopped clove of garlic

TIMING

Just before the unfavorable positions occur

THE SPELL

* Push the paper right down into the jar, saying, *These unfortunate stars in my life I repel. This day/period my fortunes shall go well. Banished be, effects that might be bad for me.*

* Add in the threads and the chopped garlic so that the jar is packed.

* Seal and bury it in a marked place until the star positions become favorable.

* Dig it up and dispose of the jar and its contents intact.

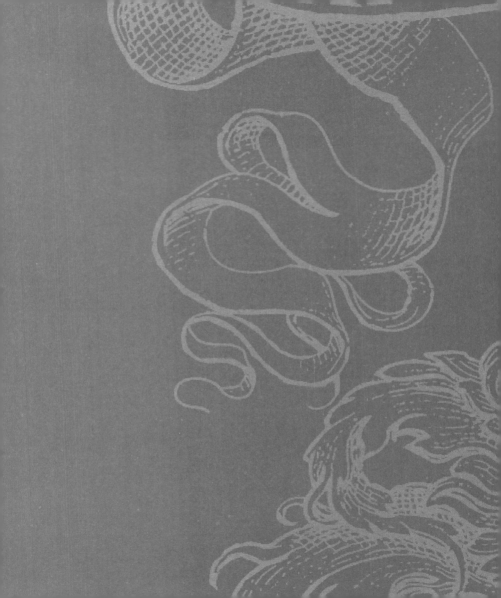

CHAPTER 2

Protection FROM AND Wards Against Paranormal Attack

I f you are psychic you will already be aware of spirit energies everywhere. What is more, if you live or work in premises that are built on or near lines of energy, such as ley lines, Irish fairy paths, indigenous American Indian ancient straight roads dating from more than thousand years ago, or Australian aboriginal spirit song lines, you may be disturbed by wandering spirits who may not be malicious but are following their traditional paths and have no consideration for your peace or privacy.

Bad events in your home before you moved in or on the land can hold restless earthbound spirits, and children can be especially upset by seeing a strange person in their bedroom at night, even if it's a family ancestor. Even more sinister, teenagers or adults who dabble with séances or Ouija boards may attract low-life spirits who follow them home and refuse to leave.

This chapter contains rituals against every form of haunting, including poltergeists and evil spirits, and includes the traditional technique of creating magical "wards," or psychic exclusion zones and "wardens," objects empowered to act as protective guardians to keep out negative spirits.

An Iron Protection Ritual to Keep Away All Evil Spirits from Your Home

YOU WILL NEED

A hammer ✳ Twelve new iron or steel nails
✳ Four small pieces of wood

TIMING

The first day of the month

THE SPELL

✳ Face approximate north (use a compass or estimate the direction). Hammer three nails into one piece of wood, left to right, saying continuously, *I hammer in protection, in all directions. May no entity or spirit bringing harm, cross these bounds, defy this charm.*

✳ Attach the wood to an interior or exterior wall in the approximate north of the home, saying, *Set and bound, this magical ward, from the north no spirit may break through this guard.*

✳ Hammer three nails in each of the other three pieces of wood and set in approximate east, then south, then west, adapting the second set of words for each direction.

To Remove a Spirit that is Frightening Your Children at Night

YOU WILL NEED

The Michael, archangel of the sun, protective sigil
(an inscribed or painted symbol considered
to have magical power) ✳ A red candle
✳ A small crystal angel for each child

TIMING

When the child(ren) are not home

ARCHANGEL
MICHAEL SIGIL

THE SPELL

✳ Go into each child's room and trace invisibly with your index finger the Michael sigil on the unlit candle.

✳ Light the candle in the center of the room and say, *You, whatever or whoever you are or seek, you may not stay here even another week.*

✳ Trace invisibly with your index finger the Michael sigil on the candle, on the inside of the windows, door in the room, and on the crystal angel, saying, *Michael, of this space be Warden, through this angel be my child* [Name] *Guardian. Go to the Light, Spirit, depart from here. My child you shall not fill with fear.*

✳ Hide the angel in the room or give it to the child.

If You Suspect Your Teenager or a Vulnerable Family Member is Dabbling with Ouija Boards or Going to Unsupervised Séances

YOU WILL NEED

A jasmine or myrrh incense stick ★ A silver charm or piece of jewelry for the teenager or adult ★ The sigil of Gabriel, archangel of the moon and nurturing

ARCHANGEL
GABRIEL SIGIL

TIMING

The full moon

THE SPELL

* Light the incense, passing the charm through the smoke seven times.

* Draw the Gabriel sigil over the jewelry in incense stick smoke, saying, *Gabriel let no harmful spirit penetrate this wall of love, keep shut the door between the worlds, let no evil be unfurled, from below, around, above.*

* Leave the incense to burn through and give the charm/jewelry to the teenager/vulnerable person.

* Whenever you suspect the person will be dabbling in the paranormal, draw the Gabriel sigil as he or she leaves, saying, *Keep shut the door between the worlds, let no evil be unfurled.*

Candle Protection if You Fear Paranormal Attacks and Evil Entities at Night

YOU WILL NEED

Three dark purple candles in a row in holders
★ Three white candles flat on the table

TIMING

After dark

THE SPELL

* Light the purple candle at left, saying, *Be gone all specters of evil with the shining of this light. Ended is your power to terrify me, I call on the powers of light.*

* Light the purple candle in the middle, then the purple candle at right, and say, *Evil entities, your powers will cease with the dimming of these lights, begone you specters of evil, begone into perpetual night.*

* Extinguish the first purple candle (the one at left) and replace it by lighting a white one, saying, *Illumine the way from evil to goodness.*

* Do the same for the second purple candle (in the middle), saying for white candle 2, *Show the way from darkness to light,* and for the third white candle, *That all fears may be exorcised and banished from my sight.*

* Dispose of the purple candles and let the white ones burn through.

To Remove an Incubus (Male)
or a Succubus (Female) Sexual Demon
Who Attacks While You Sleep

YOU WILL NEED

For an incubus, a spiral shell ✳ For a succubus, a round
whorl-like shell ✳ A small hollow cardboard tube with
a lid ✳ Nine sharp cloves or thorns ✳ Red thread

TIMING

10 P.M., while you are wide awake

THE SPELL

✳ Hold the shell and twist it hard between your hands, saying, *Vile demon,
while I sleep, no longer attack, your power over me no more you shall keep,
I take my power back.*

✳ Push the shell into the tube. Add the nine thorns or cloves, put on
the lid, wind the thread around the tube, and shake the tube nine times,
saying, *Tangled and mangled, with fierce barbs strangled, assault me
no more, now you know the score.*

✳ Shut the tube in a dark cupboard overnight and in the bright light
of day, throw the tube away.

To Divert an Existing Spirit Path that Passes Through Your Home if You Seem to Get Lots of Random Mischievous Spirits You Can't Identify

YOU WILL NEED

An iron stake or bracket, one for each side of the front and back doors, from a DIY or home improvement store ★ A small weatherproof bowl or dish on either side of the front and back doors

TIMING

Before sunset

THE SPELL

❋ Hammer the iron into the ground, so no sharp points can harm animals or small children.

❋ As you do this say, *Above, around, below the ground, find your way round, you Spirits on your journeys, these paths my home inside, do you misguide, and make you lose your way, go round instead this other better way.*

❋ Place regular offerings in the bowls to appease the wandering spirits—flowers, seeds, nuts—and keep the bowls well cleansed and filled, saying, *I make to you these offerings, asking your new paths joy will bring.*

If a Nasty Poltergeist or Spirit is Threatening You in Your Home

YOU WILL NEED

A new broom ✳ Four brown candles, one in each corner
of the main affected room, or the one you most live in
✳ A white candle in the center of the room

TIMING

Before sunset

THE SPELL

✳ Sweep away from the center of the room through the whole house,
  if affected, to the front door, saying, *I sweep all evil from this home,
  malevolent spirits, elsewhere roam.*

✳ Open the door and sweep all the bad energies out, putting the broom,
  bristles facing upward, just outside the front door. Slam the door.

✳ Light all the candles, starting with the corner nearest north, clockwise,
  and finally in the center, saying, *I call the guardians of this place,
  to remove all evil presences without trace.*

✳ Leave the candles to burn through.

✳ Light new candles weekly to prevent any evil from returning.

A Protection Sachet to Keep
Evil Spirits from Your Home

A small red bag or purse ★ Small quantities of three of the
following: crystallized candied angelica, dried rosemary, nettles,
sage, parsley, and vetivert ★ Salt ★ A long piece of red thread

TIMING

Saturday after dark

THE SPELL

* Open the purse and add a little of each herb plus salt, saying for each,
  Evil spirits, repelled you be, this bag denies you entry, no more trouble me.

* Tie the top of the bag or purse with three thread knots, saying, *Three by
  three, outside remain, within these walls, no presence gain, excluded be.*

* Open the front door and swing the bag fast over your head ten times,
  saying fast and loud ten times, *I expel you now. Cast from here, ejected,
  removed, begone evil and fear.*

* Throw it outside on the tenth call.

* Hang the bag on a bush or tree, or, if you live in an apartment,
  on a large plant outside the front door.

A Spirit Trap to Remove an Evil or Restless Spirit from Your Home or Workplace

YOU WILL NEED

A purple candle ✳ A small glass jar with a lid ✳ A long
piece of jewelry chain or several old tangled necklaces

TIMING

In complete darkness except for the candle

THE SPELL

✳ Light the candle and open the jar, half filling it with tangled chains
so they reach the edges and bottom of the jar, saying, *Like moth
to flame, draw close, draw near, restless Spirit enter here.*

✳ Leave the open jar in the center of the room, closing the doors
and all windows as you leave. Let no one go into the room.

✳ Enter the room in the morning, and close the door. Clap nine times
at the entrance, while pressing the lid firmly on the jar. Open the door
and windows, then take the jar to bury beneath bushes or a tree
away from your home.

To Remove and Keep Away Troubled or Malevolent Spirits from Your Home or the Land on Which It is Built, if There Have Been Bad Experiences Over the Years

YOU WILL NEED

A long stick to trace a labyrinth
(known to confuse and
keep away malevolent spirits)

TIMING

Friday morning

THE SPELL

* Inside and outside your front door, using the stick, you will draw an invisible small labyrinth as shown in here.

* Begin with a shepherd's crook shape.

* Next, draw a broken circle around the inner circle.

* Draw another broken circle around the first, leaving the gap on the opposite side.

* Draw another circle, again broken on the opposite side.

* Draw another broken circle.

* Close the pattern with a final broken circle.

* As you draw the labyrinth, say softly and continuously,
  *Round and round within these coils, forever to be circling,
  peace shall only be found, when you, Spirit, cease your troubling.*

* After twenty-four hours, sweep the invisible inner labyrinth
  through the front door, repeating the same words.

* Close the front door. The outside labyrinth will prevent
  the return of evil.

To Banish a Troublesome Poltergeist from Your Home or Workplace

YOU WILL NEED

A bowl of water in which you have swirled six pinches of salt
★ A string of bells, such as Tibetan bells, a drum, or a rattle

TIMING

Morning, preferably in sunlight

THE SPELL

* Open the doors and windows.

* Sprinkle the salted water through every room, including corners, doors, around furniture and window ledges, saying, *I mean you no ill, but your energy brings ill will, your noise and obstruction, cause me destruction. You must depart forever, come back never.*

* Ring the bells, drum, or rattle loudly around the whole area, chanting the words louder and louder until, when you reach the outermost door, make a final bang or ring and say a final *Never* as you close the door.

* Reopen it to throw out the remaining salt water and salt, then close it firmly, repeating *Never.*

To Quiet a Benign But Noisy
Deceased Relative in Your Home

YOU WILL NEED

A prelit white candle in a glass holder ✳ A vase of flowers
loved by the Spirit ✳ A photograph or an item
belonging to the deceased relative

TIMING

When everyone is in bed

THE SPELL

✳ Sit at the kitchen table in candlelight with the flowers
  on the table and hold the photograph or memento.

✳ Say softly, *You* [Name] *are welcome here but quietly. You disturb
  unintentionally. So softer be, that we may live in harmony.*

✳ Put the photograph or memento on the table, but still hold it, saying,
  *You are beloved to me/the family. We value your presence here truly.
  But when we sleep, please less intrusive be, that we may live in unity.*

✳ Transfer the still burning candle to a side table in the hallway or a
  relaxing area, adding the vase of flowers and the memento to the shrine.
  In future days, place other family ancestral mementos, photographs,
  and flowers on the side table.

A Fetter Binding if You Sense a Spirit Trying to Take Possession of You or a Loved One

YOU WILL NEED

A bowl of water and a bowl of salt ⋆ A silver-colored knife ⋆ A black pillar-shaped stone ⋆ A sacred symbol pendant with significance for you, on a chain ⋆ A small chain and an open padlock without a key

TIMING

At sunrise

THE SPELL: PART 1

❊ Add three pinches of salt to the water, and with the knife, make a cross or a sacred symbol of relevance to you on the surface of the water, saying, *I call on the protection of Light, the angels and archangels* [add any divinities or sacred sources you wish], *to deliver me* [or the person being protected] *from demon, devil, and all evil who seek to steal my* [or their] *soul. I am myself and I am whole.*

❊ Sprinkle the black pillar with salt water and wrap the chain around it, closing the padlock and saying, *So do I fetter anything seeking to possess, enter, or control my* [or name the person's] *soul. I am myself and I am whole.*

❊ Put the fettered pillar outside the door until the end of Part 2.

❊ Dig a very deep hole and bury the fettered pillar or take it to a landfill site.

THE SPELL: PART 2

* Add three more pinches of salt to the water and again make the sign of the cross or sacred symbol on the surface.

* Sprinkle salt water around the sacred symbol pendant, saying, *May all the angels, archangels, and powers of light* [name other divinities] *stand guard for me by day and night, for none shall ever possess my soul* [or name the person]. *I am myself and I am whole.*

* Wear the symbol or give it to the person in need to wear always.

* Tip the remaining salt and salt water under a running tap.

CHAPTER 3

Breaking Curses
AND Ill-wishing FROM
Individuals, Families,
AND Workplaces

A curse involves words spoken in our presence or absence, wishing negative results on us, our families, or our work, whether deliberately made in malice or delivered in anger. Ill-wishing, the energy behind cursing, can continue over a period and has been described as black balls of negativity sent our way. It is often argued that if you don't know a curse has been placed on you it can't hurt you, but if you are sensitive you will be aware of negativity flowing toward you, and you will feel jittery and unwell.

Some people also believe a curse can be carried over from a past life, can be attached to land or property from generations past, or can be passed through a cursed object where you are given a present by someone who hates you, even though he may hide his feelings, for example a wedding present from an ex-partner or future in-law. I have written a separate chapter on hexes (chapter 4), a spell cast against a person, home, or organization for a specific purpose, whether by a magical practitioner paid to attack you or a malicious amateur.

An All-Purpose Anti-Curse Spell

A rotting apple * A paper bag to hold the apple

TIMING

As the sunsets

THE SPELL

* Stand on a bridge or close to deep water with the apple in the bag.
  Take out the apple and toss it into the air over the water, saying,
  Fair is foul and foul is fair, I toss your curse [name curser if known]
  into the air.

* As the rotting apple hits the water, shake the bag vigorously from
  the bridge, upside down as you hold it, and say, *In the water,
  carried away, curse do not return by night or day.*

* On the way home, drop the paper bag, still upside down, into a
  garbage bin, slamming the lid and saying, *From cursing me you*
  [name if known] *are confined, gone from my life and from my mind.*

To Take Away a Curse or Ill-Wishing by Someone We Care For

YOU WILL NEED

A wide-necked dark glass bottle with a screw-top lid ★ Dried nettles or parsley ★ Sour milk with three teaspoons of dried garlic granules added

TIMING

In dim lighting

THE SPELL

❋ Fill the bottle halfway with nettles, saying, *Sharp and wounding, my love for you in vain. No more in my life shall your curse remain.*

❋ Add the sour milk and garlic mixture until the bottle is almost full, saying, *Sour and spite, the curse is gone from sight. Though your betrayal cannot be mended, your power to hurt me henceforth is ended.*

❋ Screw on the lid and shake the bottle nine times, saying, *I would not hurt you, once dear to me, but your ill-wishing cannot be.*

❋ Pour the mix down a drain, saying, *Send not your curse ever again. I pour your power and our relationship down the drain.*

To Undo a Curse or
Ill-Wishing Spoken in Anger
by You or Someone Else

YOU WILL NEED

A long thin strip of paper and a red pen ✳ Scissors
✳ A deep fireproof dish or a pan half-filled with sand

TIMING

10 P.M., the healing hour

THE SPELL

✳ Write the curse/angry words in red on the paper.

✳ Starting with the last word, cut the word off, dropping it in the sand or soil in the dish, and say, *The words spoken in fury, wiped out from memory.*

✳ Continue from the end toward the first word, until you have cut off all the words, repeating the chant and dropping each written word into the sand or soil.

✳ Take the dish outside and set fire to the paper, saying, *Burn away, turn away, the curse consumed in flame. All shall be as before, peacefully the same.*

✳ Scatter the ashes.

To Remove Curses and Bad Karma You Believe Come from Past Worlds

YOU WILL NEED

Four myrrh incense cones on a flat heatproof
dish ★ A box with a lid, padlock, and chain
★ A bowl of dead leaves ★ Four fallen dead twigs

TIMING

Saturday evening, the day of endings

THE SPELL

※ Light the incense cones, saying, *Curses and bad karma from past worlds, are banished now through fire and air, no longer there.*

※ Open the box and place in it the dead leaves and twigs, saying, *Curses from past lives, through the mists of time, you are no longer mine.*

※ When the cones are burned through and the ash is cool, pour it into the box, put the padlock key in the box, close the box, fasten the chain and padlock, and say, *Locked away is the past. Curses and bad karma perpetually bound fast.*

※ Dig a deep hole for the box and cover it with soil, saying, *My hidden gifts from centuries gone, into my life now as blessings come.*

If a Relative Died Cursing You

A gray candle ＊ A thin-bladed screwdriver

TIMING

As near to midnight as possible

THE SPELL

* On the unlit candle, scratch with the screwdriver the name of the relative and the words REST IN PEACE. YOUR CURSE SHALL CEASE.

* Light the candle and extinguish all other lights.

* Blow softly into the candle flame, repeating the name and the spell words.

* Once the words have disappeared, not before, extinguish the candle, put it outside the door, and in the morning dispose of it.

* Remove all photos and mementos of the person and do not mention his name again.

41

If the Person Who Cursed
You Lives Nearby

A bowl of bone meal from a garden center, or
crumbly soil ★ Cayenne pepper ★ The ash of six burned
sticks or cones of sandalwood, myrrh, or pine incense.
★ A wooden clothe-spin or popsicle stick on which you
have written the name of the perpetrator and the words
CURSE RETURNED TO SENDER ★ A small cloth or paper bag

TIMING

When you won't be seen

THE SPELL

* Mix the bone meal, pepper, and ash together in a bowl, saying,
  *Your curse I return intact, your unwarranted attack. Send it not again,
  the curse is bound to you as I write your name.*

* Roll the clothespin in the mix and pour the mix in the bag,
  repeating the words.

* Take the mix to near your neighbor's home and pour it in
  her greenery or as close as possible to her home, making sure
  the clothespin is hidden.

To Break a Curse that is Affecting Your Sleep and Well-Being

YOU WILL NEED

A lemon ✳ A citrus juicer ✳ A deep bowl of salt

TIMING

Wednesday morning

THE SPELL

✱ Cut the lemon in half and squeeze the juice from half the lemon, pouring the lemon juice away under a running tap and saying, *Your sour curse has done its worst, I take away connection. Now your power has had its hour, and is blocked from all directions.*

✱ Throw the flesh and skin away in a garbage can.

✱ Press the other half of the lemon, fruit side down, so it is buried in the salt bowl.

✱ Leave it to dry out where the sun shines, saying, *Return you cannot, your curse seeps away, dried up and decayed.*

✱ When it is dry, bury it under stones or rocks and say, *Rise no more.*

To Remove a Curse That Has Been Put on Your Land or Property, Perhaps Generations Before

A compass * Eight black obsidian arrows or eight black tourmalines or any dark-colored pointed crystals * Eight small black pointed marker stones found away from the land

TIMING

First light on Sunday

THE SPELL

44

* Using the compass, with the stones mark the eight directions outside your home, beginning with north, moving counterclockwise to northwest. If you live in an apartment, use a big planter.

* Holding the pointed crystals in your open-cupped hands, say eight times, *Absorb the curse, curse rot away, henceforward from this day. Let Earth transform decay to goodness, and only goodness stay.*

* Plant the pointed crystals, points facing down, into the earth and cover them, leaving the marker stones in place.

* Once a week for a year, touch each of the marker stones clockwise and repeat the words.

To Repel a Curse Right After It is Made

YOU WILL NEED
Nothing

TIMING
Immediately after the curse is made

THE SPELL

* After or even as the words are spoken, rock back on your heels, turn away, clap, turn around again fast, pushing the air hard toward the perpetrator with your hands, even if he is walking away.

* Say, *You can have that back right away, your words I do deny. Your cursing rebounds on you this day, so I do say, three times three, returned by me. You made it, you have it, free shall I be.*

* Keep pushing away the air until he is gone. If you can't speak aloud, say the words in your mind after the curse, subtly pushing your hands toward the perpetrator until he retreats, *then* turn and clap.

Another All-Purpose Curse-Breaking Ritual

Two twigs of identical length and
thickness of rowan, oak, redwood, or any
powerful tree from your region ★ Red thread
★ A sharp instrument, such as an awl (optional)

TIMING

*Whenever you sense that you,
your home, your workplace,
or your family have been cursed*

THE SPELL

* Bind the twigs tightly in a cross with red thread, saying, *Mighty tree,
  protector be. This curse now break, your power shall make me/us safe.
  No fear or evil shall enter here.*

* If you can obtain rowan or any other red berries (keep rowan berries
  away from children as they contain the toxic parasorbic acid and
  can cause stomach aches), make a small wreath for the top of
  the cross, repeating the spell words as you thread the berries with
  a sharp instrument on red thread.

* If possible, hang the cross over and outside the front door or a
  front-facing window. If it's for work, make a miniature one and
  hide it on an inside door or even in your workspace.

* Replace it every three months.

If You are Told by a Third Person That Someone Has Placed a Curse on You

YOU WILL NEED

Water in which new iron or steel nails have been soaked
in a metal bowl for 24 hours, known magically
as warrior water ✳ Dried dill

TIMING

Within 48 hours of the curse, if possible

THE SPELL

* After soaking the nails for 24 hours, add the dill to the warrior water, saying, *By the power of iron and the power of dill, I drive back this curse where it will. To the perpetrator or messenger who stands in the way, leave me now, anyhow, anyway.*

* Take out the nails, bury them, scatter the water on your doorstep or on any hard surface near your home, and then wash it away with clean water, saying, *Warrior water, take up my cause. Flow away and take this curse.*

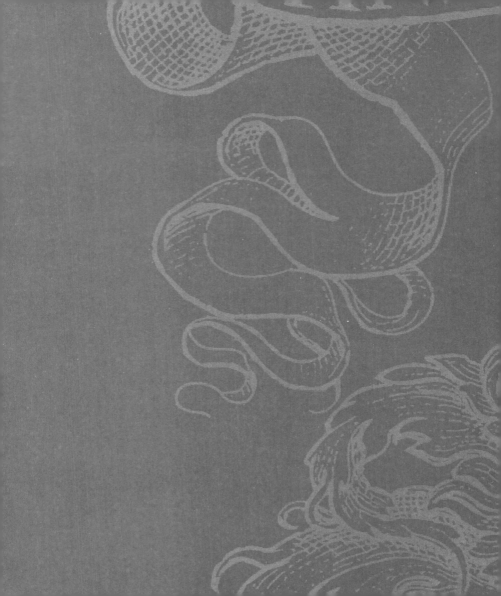

CHAPTER 4

Breaking Written AND Spoken Hexes BY Magical Practitioners, Amateur AND Professional

Hexes are more formal, deliberate, psychic attacks against a person, her home, or her workplace with the intent of bringing harm and misfortune. You will almost certainly be told by someone that you have been hexed or you may find a small doll or animal bones near the entrance to your home or even hidden within it by a malicious visitor. People may pay a magical practitioner to craft a hex against you. Amateurs, too, who dabble in black magick or belong to a negatively focused coven or psychic group, may create hexes, especially directed against those who leave their circle.

Teenagers may use dubious occult online sources to make hexes against others—a nasty form of bullying. If your teenager seems disturbed or afraid to go to bed, and you are aware that his friends dip into the dark arts, encourage him to talk. Consider doing a spell with him to have his power returned to him. For hexes can be easily broken and this breaking prevents them from being sent again.

None of the spells in this chapter return evil with evil and so are quite safe, since they are protective not aggressive. Chain mails promising good fortune can often contain a hidden hex against anyone lured in to replying by promises of love or money. But remember: those who cast hexes put themselves in a vulnerable position, for, like any bad magical sending, a hex will rebound back with three times the intensity onto the perpetrator.

To Remove a Hex Collectively Sent by a Magick or Psychic Group You Left

YOU WILL NEED

The name of your coven or psychic group, written on white paper in red ink and crossed out * A mint infusion, made with a mint tea bag steeped in boiling water for 10 minutes and strained

TIMING

Outdoors at the time the coven or group usually meets

THE SPELL

* Anchor the paper down on soil or grass, saying, *The hex and connections I return to the ground, free from above, below, around.*

* Stir the infusion nine times counterclockwise, saying, *All connections with* [name group or coven] *I now unwind. The hex against me, I do unbind.*

* Sprinkle nine counterclockwise circles of the infusion around the paper, saying, *The hex set on me, I now undo, I crush it hard beneath my shoe.*

* Jump into the circle of infusion and stamp on the paper nine times.

* Pour away any remaining infusion, burn the paper, and scatter the ashes.

If You Must Regularly See the Person Who Has Hexed You

YOU WILL NEED

A plate or glass with something nice for the perpetrator
to eat or drink * A smudge stick

TIMING

Any encounter

THE SPELL

* Subtly cross and uncross your fingers when you see the perpetrator, and say in your mind, *Uncrossed your hex, no longer vex. If I must share your company, I return the hex you gave to me.*

* Avoid eye contact and using their name.

* Touch the plate or stir the drink as you offer refreshments, and, if they refuse, brush your hand against them and afterward subtly shake your hand, saying in your mind, *This is yours I believe. Your own hex and curse now receive.*

* If you're at home afterward, smudge the house. Smudging involves burning selected herbs or other materials, or burning a smudge stick, which can be purchased from your local new-age store. Burn the smudge, walking around with it in a manner that fills the home or other space with the fragrance of the smoke and is believed to clear negative energy. If you're at work, sniff lavender oil on a tissue.

Casting a Hex to the Four Winds

A large black feather ★ A long bare stick
★ A piece of string ★ A sharp knife

TIMING

A windy day, if possible

THE SPELL

* Find an open space.

* Loosely hold the feather in your nondominant hand, so that it is shaken by the wind.

* Brush your other hand over the feather briskly, saying, *I cast this hexing to the winds, every vestige of hex is gone. Winds do what you will, its power is done.*

* Put the stick in the ground in an exposed place and tie the feather around it with the string.

* Cut the string with the knife and walk away without looking backward.

Removing a Hex That Has Tangled You into Indecision or is Draining Your Energy and Health

YOU WILL NEED

Something tangled, such as old wool or threads, or tangle
some red wool ✳ Scissors ✳ A container with a lid

TIMING

The end of a week or a month

THE SPELL

✳ Hold the tangled fibers between your hands, saying, *Into you, hex,
I now impress, the suffering caused that does me vex. Pressed into you
and free from me, I give you back this misery.*

✳ Cut with force the tangled fibers into small pieces and drop them
into the open container, making sure no knots remain.

✳ Put on the lid and say, *Untangled, my energy is my own. Hex your power
is cut and gone. I am myself, my life restored. Your evil web ties me no more.*

✳ Bury the cut wool in a compost heap, or burn it, or keep it in the sealed
container in a dark place until you have time to do so.

To Remove a Hex or Deliberate Spell Sent Against Your Home, Land, or Animals

YOU WILL NEED

Two smooth long twigs * A small basket of dying leaves

TIMING

Early on Wednesday morning, the day of Raphael the angel,
who guards against human snakes

THE SPELL

* Place the two twigs, crossed as near to your outermost property line as possible, saying, *Crossed in evil, no more shall see. Remove this hex immediately.*

* Uncross the twigs and set them side-by-side, saying, *Uncrossed from evil, connection broken, totally.*

* Cast them in different directions away from your property line in an open place, saying, *Scattered the hex, I walk away free, unvexed.*

* Scatter the dying leaves where you set the twigs to cleanse the energies as they die or blow away.

An Alternative Hex-Removing Spell
if You Need to Protect Your Home
and/or Family But Have No Land

YOU WILL NEED

A chalkboard or a flat surface on which to write
★ White chalk ★ An eraser ★ A few drops
of white vinegar or lemon juice

TIMING

Wednesday in daylight

THE SPELL

* On the board or the flat surface, draw a large chalk cross. Say, *Crossed against me, yet of your hex shall I break free, easily.*

* Rub out the cross with the eraser and draw two vertical chalk lines, side by side but not touching. Say, *Your hex loses power, hour by hour.*

* Leave the lines in place until the next morning, then erase them and clean the board or surface with warm water to which a few drops of white vinegar or lemon juice has been added, saying, *Unhexed, you who in malice sent this spell, your evil doings are dispelled. I wish you well.*

To Remove a Hex if Someone is Taunting You about Their Power over You

YOU WILL NEED

Five small, round, black stones, found near your home
* Six small, round, slightly larger white stones, found near your home * A small black bag

TIMING

Saturday afternoon

THE SPELL

* Set the stones on a table in a row, alternating black and white, starting with white.

* Remove the first black stone to the left in the row and put it in the bag, saying, *Five black stones, hexing in a row, I remove one, and so the power goes.*

* Moving right, take the next black stone and put that in the bag, saying, *Four black stones . . .* and continue the chant.

* Continue until only one remains.

* Toss the last black stone in the air, saying three times as you toss it three times, *Five, four, three, two, one, the hex is gone.*

* Put the last black stone in the bag.

* Close the bag to dispose of it in any way you choose, following the spell.

* Set the six white stones along an indoor window ledge and leave them there.

To Take Away a Hex from a Small Item That Has Been Sent as a Gift

YOU WILL NEED

The small item you wish to protect ★ If the item is
delicate, a cloth in which to wrap it ★ An old
bowl ★ Salt ★ A large black stone

TIMING

During the waning moon

THE SPELL

* Put the item in the bowl, saying, *Hex, you are deactivated, disempowered, and neutralized. You are banished from my life and cut down to size. Hex, you shall be buried, and can no longer rise.*

* Press salt all around it, so the item is totally immersed, and put the stone on top of it, so the bowl is completely filled and the item is completely covered, saying, *The hex cannot move, ineffective does it prove.*

* Leave the stone and the bowl at the back of a dark cupboard until the crescent moon when, if you wish to keep the item, it is safe. Preferably bury it and put the stone as an anchor on top where no plants grow.

To Undo a Hex Sent as a Poison Pen Letter or a Chain Email from an Untraceable Source

YOU WILL NEED

A printout of the email or the letter ⋆ A blue waterproof marker pen ⋆ An envelope

TIMING

Soon after receiving it

THE SPELL

* Hold the printout of the email or the letter between your hands and say, *Not worth the paper it is written/printed on, I block out this hex and it is done.*

* Set it on a flat surface, preferably outdoors, and, starting at the bottom right and moving left and then left to right and upward, color totally over the words in blue pen, saying, *Overwritten, obliterated, covered, the hex with blue now is smothered.*

* When it is dry, fold it, put it in an envelope, and seal the envelope, writing, RETURN TO SENDER on the front.

* Rip the envelope and its contents into pieces and drop the pieces in a recycling bin.

To Unhex a Large Item You Must Keep

Eight long leafless twigs

Morning as light returns

* Outdoors, if possible, place two crossed sticks at each corner of the object, saying, *Cross, cross, crossing, soon to be uncrossed, and then all your power is lost.*

* Starting in the corner nearest to you and moving counterclockwise, uncross and break each pair of twigs.

* Afterward, collect the twigs in a bundle, toss them in the air as far as possible from the item (if necessary, indoors from a window), saying, *Hex hex, go away, forbidden to return here any day.*

* The item is now free.

60

If You Know a Powerful Practitioner
Has Been Employed to Hex You

YOU WILL NEED

Nine hairs cut from your head or from your
hairbrush ∗ A strong long red thread

TIMING

Dawn on Sunday

THE SPELL

∗ Knot the hairs individually at regular intervals along the thread,
   if necessary using extra pieces of thread to attach them. Say,
   *My power I reclaim as my own, my energies to my enemies are no more
   known. I bind and wind my soul secure, the hex no longer shall endure.*

∗ Burn the hairs and thread, saying, *Out of Sight, out of mind, my essence
   you can no longer find. Guardians of the fire hold safe my power, and on
   me your protection shower.*

If You Find a Sending in Your Home, Workspace, or Land, Such as a Doll, Animal Bones, a Dead Small Animal, or Crossed Sticks

Note: A sending is an unpleasant or evil thing or creature sent by someone with paranormal or magical powers to warn, punish, or take revenge on a person

YOU WILL NEED

The sending ★ An old cloth ★ Red string

TIMING

Soon after you find it or, if not, keep it wrapped until you can cast the spell

THE SPELL

* Pick up the sending, wrapped in the cloth, and wrap it firmly with three knots of the string, saying, *This sending do I bind with string. This sending is a rejected thing. So I return and do undo, your attempted hex, sent back to you.*

* Find a crossroads, on a road, at an intersection of paths, or create a three-stick formation in a circle in your garden or a planter, making the protective Celtic awen symbol (see drawing).

* Bury the sending, saying, *At the crossroads of destiny, buried in obscurity, your sending now shall be. No more to trouble me.*

If Amateurs Have Been Dabbling in the Dark Arts and Hexed Your Teenager or Another Family Member Out of Spite

YOU WILL NEED

A small item belonging to your teenager or other family member ✴ Rose or lavender potpourri ✴ Dried sage ✴ Three gold Archangel Michael candles

TIMING

Sunday

THE SPELL

* Place the small item in a circle of rose or lavender potpourri.

* Scatter the dried sage in a square around the circle of potpourri.

* Place the Michael candles in a triangle around the square.

* Light the three Michael candles, moving clockwise from the one nearest you, saying for each one, *Michael, guardian of the light, protect* [Name] *from those who play with darkness out of spite.*

* Blow softly into each candle, saying for the first one, *Michael,* for the second, *Protect,* and for the third, *From darkness with your light.*

* Extinguish the candles, saying, *Extinguished the hex by the power of light, wiped out is evil, destroyed spite.*

* The sufferer may benefit from doing the spell with you and wearing or carrying the item, especially at night.

CHAPTER 5

Protection FROM Bullying, Abuse, AND Intimidation, Both Physical AND Psychological

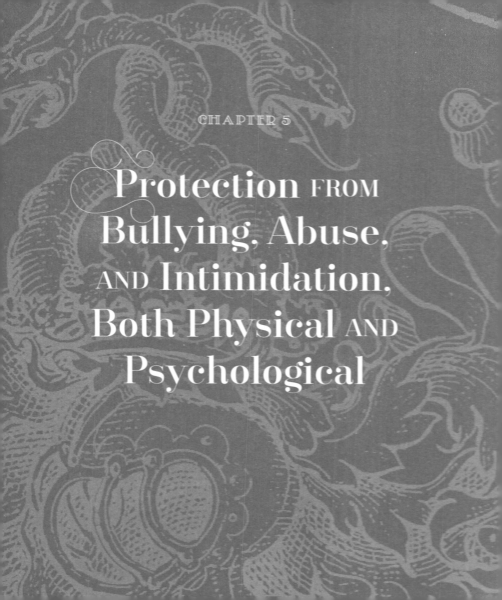

Spells, however powerful, are not a substitute for action or seeking official or legal help in the everyday world. However, they strengthen any efforts you do make, practically or legally, and protect you from and reduce the negative effects of the abuse you are receiving while the abuse is being addressed by authorities.

However, justice can be blind or bullies so well protected or hide their abuse so well at work, at school, or in society that your efforts at getting relief may be ignored and you or a suffering child may be blamed for causing problems. In these cases, magick will erect defensive shields or psychic exclusion zones (wards) around you and loved ones and work to bind or banish bullies.

The spells in this chapter act directly against the bully under the threefold law of returning nastiness to its perpetrator and all strengthen the aura energy field of the sufferer so they give off powerful *Don't mess with me vibes* that may turn the bully's attention away. What is more, a spell may expose a bully for what he really is and so lead to worldly action against him.

A Mars Iron Protection Ritual When You are Being Bullied and No One Listens

YOU WILL NEED

Seven paper clips, each stretched out and
ends crossed, the metal of Mars ∗ Seven dragon's
blood incense sticks or incense sticks of any
spice, set upright in a deep dish of soil

TIMING

Tuesday for seven nights

THE SPELL

* The first night, light the first incense stick, standing upright in the soil. Bury beneath it the first paper clip, saying, *Defend me against bullying and rage. Mars, I ask, bring strength and courage.*

* Leave the incense to burn through, burying the ash in the soil.

* Each night repeat the spell with the next incense stick and paper clip.

* On night 7, after burying the seventh paper clip, plunge the still-lighted incense stick downward into the soil, saying, *By Mars's iron will, you are barred from here, never more to intimidate me or cause fear.*

* When cold, pour the contents of the dish into a hole in the earth.

Countering Bullying and Destructive Behavior Directed Against You by Family Members

YOU WILL NEED

Seven small sharks' teeth or small sharp chicken bones
★ A small red bag ★ Dried tarragon, the dragon's herb

TIMING

Tuesday, as early in the day as possible

THE SPELL

※ Place the sharks' teeth in the bag one at a time, saying for each one, *Bite not the hand that feeds you. Speak not viciously against me who tells you true. Resist, desist your words of spite. Act not in ways that are not right. This unkind behavior cannot be. Seven times I turn your unkindness back from me.*

※ Add seven pinches of the dragon's herb to the bag, one at a time, saying the spell words for each pinch.

※ Close and shake the bag seven times, again saying the spell words.

※ Hide the bag near the front door and when you are expecting any of the nasty people, take it out, shake it seven times and repeat the spell words.

To Thwart Direct Threats and Intimidation Directed Toward a Teenager or Child at School or in Social Situations

YOU WILL NEED

Cayenne pepper, cinnamon, ginger, and garlic granules ✳ A metal bowl and a small wooden meat tenderizer ✳ The first name(s) of the bully/bullies written in black on red paper, all the names joined together and vowels removed ✳ Dragon's blood oil

TIMING

Tuesday in daylight

THE SPELL

✳ Mix the herbal ingredients in the metal bowl, pounding them hard and saying forcefully, *You, threaten not* [name child], *nor intimidate. Stop this hate. This bullying must cease, instantly. Hear me and fear. I am near.*

✳ Cut the paper into tiny pieces and mix it in with a few drops of oil, saying, *Aggressiveness now is quenched. From bullying ways you now are wrenched.*

✳ Wash the mix away outdoors under a hose or tap, down a drain, or scoop it into a waterproof bag and dump it in the garbage.

To Expose and Defeat
Well-Hidden Bullying

YOU WILL NEED

Frankincense or dragon's blood essential oil
★ A small dish ★ A thin screwdriver or a letter opener
★ A diffuser preferably with a candle beneath

TIMING

Around noon

THE SPELL

✳ Pour oil into the dish, and in the oil, trace on its surface the name of the bully/bullies with the screwdriver (instantly the words will disappear). Say, *Revealed in the light of day, soon your power will burn away.*

✳ Heat a little water in the diffuser and add the oil, a few drops at a time, saying, *Fire and light break through your veneer. Your bullying shall publicly appear, loud and clear. And as this oil burns away, your power over me loses all sway.*

✳ When the diffuser is almost dry, extinguish the candle beneath it, saying, *Hide no more your bullying ways. I face you strong and strong will stay.*

To Deter an Ex-Partner
Who Bullies You in Your Home
When Legal Means Have Failed

YOU WILL NEED

A figure made from children's modeling clay
★ Red twine or strong thread ★ A small red jasper crystal

TIMING

Tuesday noontime, if possible

THE SPELL

* Bind the figure's hands and feet with the twine, and place the crystal where the mouth should be, saying, *You are bound from bullying deed and word. Your threatening presence in my home no more shall be seen or heard.*

* Place the figure beneath the doormat and say, *Crushed your intimidation beneath my feet, trampled is your vicious heat. Barred are you from my door, or you walk over yourself and feel the score.*

To Counteract the Actions of a Person Who Bullies You Through Guilt and Obligation

YOU WILL NEED

A bowl of salt ★ A large jug of water ★ A long spoon

TIMING

Before a visit or contact

THE SPELL

※ Sprinkle a few pinches of salt in the water, while stirring it counterclockwise and saying, *Drip by drip, drop by drop, your emotional blackmail now shall stop*.

※ Pour the salty water away under a running tap, refilling the jug and adding more salt, stirring, and repeating the spell words.

※ Continue until all the salt is gone. Wash out the salt bowl and turn off the tap, saying, *Drip by drip, drop by drop, unwarranted guilt at last has stopped. False obligations no longer me enthrall, I shall deal with* [name perpetrator(s)] *on my terms or not at all.*

To Repel Unscrupulous Creditors and Loan Sharks Who Constantly Call, Text, and Send You Letters

YOU WILL NEED

A gray candle * A myrrh or musk incense stick
or a small cedar smudge stick

TIMING

Evening or on a misty day

THE SPELL

* Go where you will not be disturbed and switch off all mobile devices.

* Light the gray candle, saying, *The light grows dim, I am shielded from your view, hidden from persecution by any of you. You who ruthlessly pursue me, forget I am here, I disappear.*

* Extinguish the candle, relight it, and, lighting the smudge or incense from the candle, spiral it arm's length away, counterclockwise, saying, *Above me, below me, and down to the ground, may this cloak of invisibility shelter me around. From my persecutors who persist in harassing, no more shall their call fear bring.*

* Leave the smudge to burn away and attempt (maybe yet again) to get official help.

If You Have a Violent, Threatening Neighbor or Live in a Dangerous Area

A red candle with color all the way through ⋆ Four small,
recyclable bottles or jars with lids, set in a row
⋆ A compass ⋆ A bunch of old or rusty iron nails
⋆ Sprigs of fresh or dried rosemary ⋆ Sour red wine

TIMING

Sunset

THE SPELL

* Light the candle and work only by its light.

* Name a bottle for each compass direction, left to right, half-filling each in turn first with nails, then adding rosemary and wine, until each bottle is almost full.

* Put on each lid and shake the first bottle on the left three times, saying, *Guardian of the north, stand sentinel.*

* Shake bottle 2, while saying, *Guardian of the east, I call you as well.*
Shake bottle 3, saying, *Southern warden be for me.*
Shake bottle 4, and say, *Finally you western shield, to threats and violence do not yield.*

* When it is dark, bury each bottle in the ground or in a planter in its own compass direction, saying, *From north, east, south and west, guard me and my home against all danger, from hostile neighbor and malicious stranger.*

Another Spell to Protect a Child or Teenager Who is Being Bullied While Traveling to School or Outside of School

YOU WILL NEED

Four orange candles * An item your child/teenager carries daily * Four very small carnelians or other orange crystals

TIMING

Late evening

THE SPELL

* Place the four candles in a square.

* Place the item your child carries in the center of the square of candles.

* Light the candles, starting with the one farthest away, moving counterclockwise and saying, [Name], *be enclosed in light, in my protection, I keep you safe from all directions.*

* Hold each carnelian, in turn, in your closed hands before placing it between a candle in the square, again moving counterclockwise, saying for each, *At school, on journeys, in parks, and in stores* [add any other dangerous bullying locations], *this square acts as guardian for your cause. None may enter this zone of fire, barred be those with malicious desire.*

* Blow out the candles, creating a permanent psychic light square around the teenager/child through the item in the center.

* For added protection, sew the crystals into the lining of the child/ teenager's coat or attach the crystals, hidden, inside the bookbag he or she carries.

If You Have a Bullying Boss and You Cannot Easily Get Another Job

YOU WILL NEED

A reduced-size printed-out photo of your boss from
any source ★ Chewing gum or fix-it adhesive

TIMING

Before the workweek starts

THE SPELL

* Put the photo of your boss on your kitchen wall, saying, *Now you're not so tall, now you're not so smart. In fact you little fart, I don't fear you at all.*

* Put chewing gum or fix-it adhesive over the mouth on your boss's picture, saying, *Not so talkative now, nor critical, bullying, anyhow. Getting a laugh at my expense, nothing to say in your defense?*

* Turn the picture so that the blank side faces outward behind a cupboard door, saying, *No longer your call, now you're saying nothing at all.*

* At work if your boss starts being sarcastic, say all the spell words in your mind and stick some adhesive, facedown, on your workspace.

If You Are the Target of Bullying in a Social Group or Sports Club You Attend

YOU WILL NEED

Small, yellow jaspers, yellow beads, or glass nuggets, one representing each person in the group, excluding you ✶ A larger yellow jasper or a another larger yellow stone, representing the ringleader ✶ A gray stone, such as an agate or smoky quartz, representing you

TIMING

Before you attend

THE SPELL

* Set the small yellow beads or glass nuggets in a cirle.

* Place the larger yellow stone in the center of the circle.

* Touch each stone in the circle, in turn, counterclockwise, saying for each one, *Excluding me, shall no longer be. I will enter the very center.*

* Place your stone in the center, next to the ringleader's stone, and say, *A change of perspective, a new directive, everyone else must request to enter my sphere. Notice me positively. I am here.*

* Remove the ringleader's stone, putting it in a drawer out of sight and say, *Out you go, no longer your show.*

* When you arrive, talk confidently to the nearest person, ignoring the ringleader.

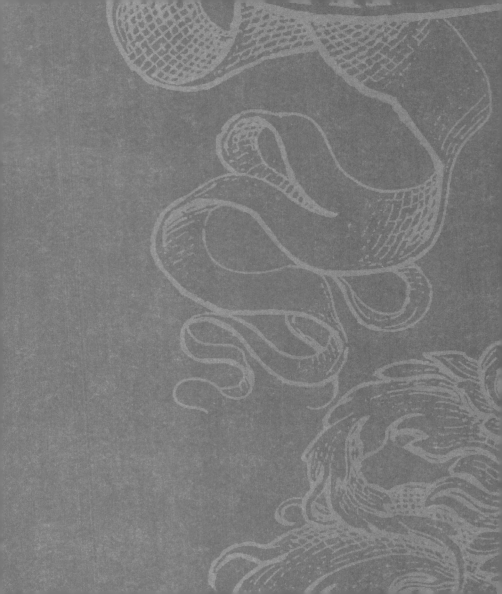

CHAPTER 6

Protection FROM Destructive AND Obsessive Love, Deception, Stalkers, AND Always Loving THE Wrong People

Love is a two-edged sword. At its best, it is devoted, caring, and lasting, enriching our lives by the presence of a soul mate. However, it can also be a trap if we love too much and always return to the same partner who promises to change, but hurts us yet again. What is more, if we cannot let go of an old love that can be no more, or one that can never be at all, we can remain trapped in false hopes and impossible dreams and never move forward.

You may be plagued by an overattentive would-be lover who will not take no for an answer or a love who won't commit but keeps you dangling in hope of *maybe one day* or an ex-partner who doesn't want you but won't let anyone else have you. Family members or a close friend can sabotage every new relationship with their possessiveness, so you end up alone. For if love becomes destructive, it tangles you in the past, preventing you from moving forward to new love and a fulfilling life. The spells in this chapter help us overcome unconscious self-sabotaging of our happiness; keep us from loving the wrong person or loving too much, regardless of the pain it causes us; and frees us from those who stand in the way of our finding lasting happiness with the right person. Therefore, they are very positive and, as a result of doing them, you will find that the right love comes and stays with you seemingly spontaneously, and commitment grows as you open your energy field to finding and keeping that right person.

If You Can't Let Go of a Love Who Keeps Returning to Your Life, But Never Changes

YOU WILL NEED

One red candle ∗ Two blue ones ∗ A thin-bladed screwdriver or a letter opener

TIMING

For seven days

THE SPELL

∗ Place the red candle between the two blue ones.

∗ On the red candle draw six lines at equal intervals to make seven divisions.

∗ Light the red candle for the destructive relationship, saying, *You, my love will never change. Though promises you make, you always break them and my heart. And so I must for my own sake, you permanently estrange.*

∗ Light the two blue candles, representing the two of you separately from the red flame, saying, *You must go your way, I shall go mine. Separately, it must be.*

∗ Leave the first notch to burn down and extinguish the red candle, saying, *My love for you I now let go, regretfully I must say no.*

∗ Blow out the two blue candles.

∗ Repeat the spell for six more days.

∗ On day 7 leave the red and blue candles to burn away.

If a Close Friend or Family Member Always Sabotages Every New Relationship You Have

YOU WILL NEED

A piece of elastic * Three small modeling clay figures,
with the sabotage doll in the middle * Scissors
or a sharp knife * A red ribbon

TIMING

Before any contact involving your new love

THE SPELL

* Tie the elastic around the figure representing you and the figure representing the close friend/relative/saboteur and say, *Puppet on a string, you cannot let me go. Wrecking with your too-loving sledgehammer, every new love I know.*

* Stretch the elastic between the two figures, then cut the elastic close to the saboteur so your figure is freed.

* Retie the elastic loosely around the saboteur figure and bind yourself to your new love with ribbon, saying, *Together shall we love willingly, stay together forever, if right it is to be.*

* Keep the figures of you and your new love in a bedside drawer and cut the saboteur figure free, rerolling it into a ball of clay.

To Free Yourself from an Ex-Partner Who Won't Move Out of Your Life

YOU WILL NEED

A long, trailing plant frond, wrapped several times around the stems of a bunch of dark yellow flowers ∗ A sharp knife ∗ A basket

TIMING

Sunday morning

THE SPELL

∗ Unwind the plant, saying, *Though the roots were deep, yet now they are gone. We are no longer one. I must go forward, as must you alone.*

∗ Cut the frond into small pieces and drop them into the basket, along with the now freed flowers.

∗ Find fast-flowing water and one by one drop the pieces of the plant from the basket into the water, saying, *Find another love and life. I must my new path make. Flow from me, go from me, set me free, for both our sakes.*

∗ Walk away and don't look back.

To Deter a Stalker if the Law is Not Being Much Help

YOU WILL NEED

A small jug of water with white vinegar added ★ A small bowl of soil ★ A small bowl of salt ★ An empty pot ★ A scoop or a large spoon for mixing ★ A bucket of water and pine cleaner and a mop or scrubbing brush

TIMING

Early morning

THE SPELL

* Mix all the water, soil, and salt together in the pot so the mix is moist but still crumbly.

* Sprinkle some of the mixture on the doorstep or in front of your home/building, saying, *You, stalker, walk, you cannot come near. Within magick exclusion, you may not trouble my seclusion. Step right back from here.*

* Scrub or mop the doorstep clean, saying, *You, stalker, walk, not to call, not to lurk, during the day or after dark, not to send, not to phone. This is my exclusion zone.*

* Pour the mixture down the drain, saying, *Washed away, into my presence you cannot stray. Stalker, walk.*

If You Always Attract
Users and Losers in Love

YOU WILL NEED
Two dice

TIMING
Wednesday, the lucky day

THE SPELL

* Shake the dice vigorously in closed-cupped hands, saying (while tossing faster and faster), *Losers and users, you who love power, you who cheat, lie and make true love sour, be gone from my life, end all my love strife.*

* When you can chant and toss no faster, roll the dice and continue to chant, toss and roll until you get two sixes.

* Then say, *Jackpot in love, only true love apply. Be faithful forever. Respect me, adore me, or else pass on by.*

* Carry the dice with you when you go on a date or somewhere socially. Before leaving your home, shake them three times and say three times, *Jackpot in love, only true love apply. Be faithful forever. Respect me, adore me, or else pass on by.*

If Your Love is Leading a Double Life or Has Major Secrets S/he Keeps from You

YOU WILL NEED

Two identical photos of your love ★ Three white
candles ★ Three dark-colored candles ★ Glue

TIMING

A clear day

THE SPELL

* Place the photos side by side.

* Behind the photos, alternate the white and dark-colored candles in a row.

* Light each dark-colored candle in turn, saying, *Either commit to me fully, or depart. I do not want half your heart.*

* Now light the white ones, saying, *Half and half, a double life. Be honest with me and end this strife.*

* Put one photo on top of the other, face-to-face and glue them together, saying, *Come to me wholeheartedly, or go forever. For your hidden world must now ended be, I will accept it never.*

* Extinguish only the dark candles and rip up the glued photos, saying, *Two of you, we start anew, free from deceit and secrecy. Total honesty is due, or we are through.*

* State your terms when next you meet and accept no compromise.

To Prevent Your Partner from Having an Affair If You Know S/he is Tempted

YOU WILL NEED

A red candle * A dragon's blood incense stick
for temptation * A bowl of sand * A blue
candle * A lavender incense stick for fidelity

TIMING

When you know temptation will arise

THE SPELL

* Light the red candle, saying, *Burn away fire, this false desire. Put out the flame of the one I shall not name.*

* Light the dragon's blood incense stick, saying, *The brief power of lust, be destroyed you must. For our love is long, and can once more grow strong.*

* Extinguish the red candle, saying, *No false passions shall remain, I quench the flame.*

* Plunge the burning incense into the sand and crush it, saying, *Dry as the desert sand.*

* Light the blue candle and the lavender incense and leave them to burn through.

* Throw away the sand and the red candle.

If Your Partner is Abusive But You're Afraid to Leave

YOU WILL NEED

A token of the relationship ★ As heavy a stone
as you can lift, found near water ★ String

TIMING

Near any still water, early in the morning

THE SPELL

* Go to the water while holding the token, say, *The burden I bear is heavy. Yet to let go I hesitate.*

* Lift the stone, saying, *I feel the weight.*

* Attach the token to the stone with string and throw the stone into the water, saying, *Burden me no more.*

If You Yearn for an Unattainable Lost Love That Keeps You from Having a Realistic Relationship

YOU WILL NEED

A yellow rosebud, to represent your unattainable love
* Two pieces of blotting paper or strong printer paper

TIMING

Saturday, as darkness falls

THE SPELL

* Press the flower between the pieces of paper, saying, *My love can remain only in memory. Fade it must and leave me free.*

* Put the pieces of paper containing the rosebud between the pages of an old, heavy book you never read as it may make the pages wrinkle, for a minimum of seven to ten days.

* Then, if you are ready, dispose of the pressed flower or leave it there until you feel fully able to let go.

* Plant or buy flowers of another kind and color to represent the future.

89

If Your Love Must Stay Hidden Because of Opposition or Because the Relationship Will Hurt Others

YOU WILL NEED

A white silk rose, the symbol of secret love

TIMING

Saturday, after dark

THE SPELL

* Into the rose, whisper the name of your love and the words, *Within this rose does my hidden love lie, a love so deep it will never die, a love though it can never be spoken, yet never shall or can be broken.*

* Repeat the words in a softer and softer voice, until they fall into silence.

* Do this every Saturday until the flower discolors, then replace it if secrecy is still necessary.

If an Unwanted Admirer, Known or Unknown, Bombards You with Gifts

YOU WILL NEED

Chalk * One of the gifts

TIMING

The end of a day, week, or month

THE SPELL

* Place the gift on a surface on which you are able to draw with chalk.

* Draw a chalk circle counterclockwise around the gift, saying, *Your gifts are kind, but I am not for sale. You buy me in vain, I remove you from my life and mind, send not again.*

* Rub out the circle clockwise, saying, *The connection through your offerings, regrettably to an end I bring. With this erasing I erase your attention. Think no more of me, neither contact nor mention.*

* If you have a mailing address for the sender, return the presents with a note saying that you thank the sender but cannot accept the gifts and please make no more contact. If the admirer is unknown, give the gifts to charity.

If Leaving a Bad Relationship Will Be Financially Disastrous

THE SPELL

* Strand by strand, unravel the embroidery silk and take just one long
strand. Shredding or cutting the rest of the separate threads, say,
*I unravel my old life that causes me pain. Though I leave all wealth behind,
myself I shall find.*

* Put the shredded threads into the box, put on the lid, and hide it in a
dark space in the place you are leaving, saying, *Possessions and money
call me in vain, I shall not return here ever again.*

* Thread small shiny beads on the remaining strand, knot it, and hang it
in your new abode where the sun shines.

If Your Teenager is Obsessed with a Much Older Partner or One with Destructive Habits

YOU WILL NEED

White paper ★ A white ink pen or crayon ★ A black pen ★ A magnifying glass ★ An elastic band ★ A double-sided mirror

TIMING

Any day before they see each other

THE SPELL

* Write the name of the undesirable love in white on white paper, saying, [name of teenager], *Obsessed by dreams, in love with love, blinded by illusion, all is not as it seems.*

* Write over the name in black ink, saying, *Beloved child, you are blinded by youth. Look through my eyes and see clearly the truth.*

* Hold the magnifying glass closer and closer to the name until the letters blur, saying, *Truth hurts, But illusion blurs. My child with clear eyes, act wise. Ahead of you lies the rest of your life. Don't settle for strife.*

* Wrap the paper, secured with an elastic band, and attach it to the back of a double-sided mirror on the wall.

CHAPTER 7

Protection FROM Cyberbullying, Social Media Nastiness, Online Dating Hazards, AND Internet Fraud

he internet has introduced us to worldwide friendships, an information superhighway, and online dating. Increasing numbers of people are meeting their soul mates online. The energies of the internet seem to closely mirror the old magical channels of lighting a candle and asking for what you want or calling love. However, the internet also opens channels for vicious and widespread online bullying, especially directed at vulnerable teenagers; brings together through dating sites less than reputable people, claiming to be what they are not; and promotes financial scams of all kinds. What is more, so-called internet trolls post vicious comments about happy events or requests for healing blessings, not just to the rich and famous, but to ordinary people who are sharing their good fortune online with the best of motives and may hardly be known to the trolls.

Since sometimes actually blocking nastiness on social media is only partially successful in ridding yourself of online viciousness, the spells in this chapter work to bar and, under magical law, return threats and nastiness. They also protect internet users, both social and professional, from the hazards of online communication.

To Prevent Social Media Nastiness by Trolls

YOU WILL NEED

The computer or other device you use to access social media
sites * A dark-colored candle * A candle snuffer

TIMING

Five consecutive nights

THE SPELL

* Switch on your computer or the device through which you receive troll messages and call up troll comments or a major troll's social media page.

* Light the candle on the other side of the room and switch off all other lights.

* Looking at the screen, say, *Trolls, your vicious souls reach out through cyberspace. But day by day your power will be diminished, your evil reign soon will be finished. Five, four, three, two, one, gone. Put in your place.*

* Clap five times and extinguish the candle with the snuffer.

* Repeat the spell exactly as above for four more days and then do some serious blocking of any nasty connections.

If Your Internet Lover Constantly Puts Off Meeting You

98

YOU WILL NEED

The device/computer through which you communicate ★ Rose petals

TIMING

Before you connect online

THE SPELL

* Put your pictures side by side on your screen and enclose them in an onscreen heart.

* Move the pictures so they merge into one onscreen, still within the heart, saying, *Come to me in reality, speak to me actually. Not just meeting in cyberspace, but face-to-face. If there is nothing to conceal, yourself reveal.*

* Print out the merged images and heart, and cover the printout with rose petals, saying, *Come to me now, anywhere, anyhow. Emerge from within the safety screen, so you may for your true self be seen.*

* Scatter the petals outdoors and put the image in front of the screen as you make contact.

If a Former Friend or Ex-Partner is Stirring Up Trouble Against You on Social Media

YOU WILL NEED

A printout of the latest message and photos
* A thick green permanent marker

TIMING

Whenever a nasty message or photos appear

THE SPELL

* Beginning from the end and working backwards on a written message, letter by letter, block out in green the message until you reach the first letter. Now work on any pictures from left bottom corner to top right corner, along imaginary rows until the photo is hidden from view.

* Say continuously, *Gone, undone, without trace. I do undo, this disgraceful spitefulness from you. Blocked in green, on my computer and life never more is seen.*

* Put the paper in a shredder or rip it up into small pieces and place it into the garbage bin, saying, *Worth nothing except as garbage, send no more your spiteful messages.*

If You Suspect a Friend or Family Member is Being Scammed by an Internet Lover and Won't Heed Your Advice

YOU WILL NEED

A green and black malachite crystal or a turquoise crystal
★ A pan of cold water ★ Dried parsley and tarragon

TIMING

Wednesday, the day of overcoming fraudsters

THE SPELL

* Drop the crystal in water, saying, *High and dry, your falsehood is. May your deception, receive from* [Name] *no more loving reception.*

* Remove the crystal, add tarragon and parsley to the water and bring it to a boil.

* As steam begins to form, carefully hold the crystal in the steam for a second or two, saying, *High and dry, may* [Name] *see with clear eye, Your trickery, out of his/her life shall you be.*

* Pour the water under a cold tap so it hisses and wash out the pan.

* Give the crystal to the person being scammed or keep it with his/her photo.

A Waxing and Full Moon Spell if You're Applying for an Online Loan or Credit Card and Have Previously Been Rejected

YOU WILL NEED

Four pearls or pearl buttons ★ A hollow shell near the computer or other electronic device you will be using

TIMING

From the crescent to the night before the full moon, unless the need is urgent, in which case any two consecutive nights

THE SPELL

* Drop the pearls into the shell one by one, saying, *Look on me favorably, that I may no longer rejected be, by the right online finance company.*

* On full moon night, if possible outdoors, cast three of the pearls as far as you can, saying, *Lady Moon my offering, on my computer acceptance bring.*

* Leave the remaining pearl inside the shell and apply at once online for the loan or credit card.

To Prevent Your Computer from Picking Up a Virus That Slips Through Your Protection Program

YOU WILL NEED

Four green-and-black malachite crystals, the ultimate computer protection ★ Four black obsidian arrows or dark, pointed crystals

TIMING

Any time you are concerned about getting a computer virus

THE SPELL

* Before switching on your computer, hold the four malachite crystals between your cupped hands and say, *Protecting me, against viruses, hacking, and computer infamy.*

* Set each one at a corner of the computer.

* Hold the pointed crystals, points facing the machine, in your open flat hands, saying, *Stand as my guards, with defenses so hard, that repelled shall be, all computer infamy.*

* Set them in place at equal intervals around the computer between the malachite crystals, saying, *as sentinels stay, by night and day.*

* Switch on the machine and make sure conventional virus protection is up-to-date.

To Stop Scammers from Hacking Your Online Information or Committing Internet Fraud

Note: You can repeat the spell for your other devices, including your smartphone.

YOU WILL NEED
Your computer or your main electronic device

TIMING
The first time you use the computer on a Wednesday

THE SPELL

* On the screen write small in the center, THIS IS AN EXCLUSION ZONE. NONE WITH ILL INTENT MAY THROUGH IT HONE, TO CHEAT OR SCAM, DECEIVE OR HACK. THIS SPELL SENDS ALL YOUR EVIL BACK.

* Increase the size of the letters until they fill the screen, saying, *Frauds, deceivers this space is filled, secured against your scams and hacking. This spell sends your fraudulence packing.*

* Press the DELETE button fast, saying, *In the background my guardians hide, none may my internet security break inside.*

To Protect Your Children and Teenagers from Online Predators

YOU WILL NEED

Small red crystals or stones ★ Small black crystals ★ A list
of the makes and models of your children's online devices,
written in red on white paper ★ A box with a lock and key

TIMING

When your teenager is not around

THE SPELL

* Create a circle of red crystals counterclockwise and a square of black
  crystals clockwise around the paper, saying, *Predators and deceivers, you
  impersonate and lure. You cannot enter this protected space, these defenses
  shall endure. Though wickedness you disguise through flattery and lies,
  the threefold your evil does return, I spit into your eyes.*

* Fold the paper, collect the crystals, and put them in the box.
  Lock the box and throw away the key, saying, *Locked and barred,
  against all predators.*

* Hide the box away.

To Prevent Your Mobile Devices from Being Lost or Stolen

YOU WILL NEED

All your mobile devices in one place * Enough small battery-powered electric candles to surround the devices in a circle * A mirror propped so you can see the candle circle reflected in it

TIMING

During the waning moon, after dark

THE SPELL

* Turn on each of the candles in turn clockwise, saying, *By light become connected to me, not lost, borrowed or stolen. Linked and attached magically, shimmering and golden.*

* Make a straight line of the candles, leading to the mirror from the devices, so the line of candlelight is reflected in the mirror.

* Touch each candle and the devices in turn, saying, *The pathway of light joins you to me, linked to my presence unbreakably.*

* Switch off the lights and picture a golden cord of light linking you to each device.

To Prevent Your Technological Devices from Crashing or Malfunctioning

YOU WILL NEED

Two large white feathers ★ Your devices on a
table around which you can easily move

TIMING

Wednesday, the day of Archangel Raphael, angel of technology

THE SPELL

* Holding a feather in each hand, walk around the table, first counterclockwise, then clockwise, then counterclockwise again, stamping your feet while crossing tand uncrossing the feathers over your head swinging your arms to point the feathers toward the devices, in alternating movements.

* Say softly and continuously, *Efficiently, smoothly, shall you operate, permanently without difficulty. No accidents, crashes by malfunctioning randomly sent, or maliciously meant. All shall function effortlessly.*

* Gradually lower and slow your voice and movements until they fade into stillness and silence. Keep the feathers in a jar near your main machine.

To Prevent Your Online Work or Electronic Publishing from Being Illegally or Unethically Plagiarized

YOU WILL NEED
Your computer

TIMING
Wednesday early in the day

THE SPELL

* Take the first page of something already submitted online or published electronically and add a header to it, with the words THIS WORK IS MINE, CREDITED TO ME. PLEASE DO NOT STEAL IT UNETHICALLY.

* Remove the heading and words, but every time you submit work via the internet or publish electronically, add and remove the same heading and the words on the first page.

* As you press SEND, say, *No plagiarizing, no borrowing, this is my work. No thieving, no illegal copying, please credit everything.*

* Clap nine times and repeat nine times louder and louder *Everything.*

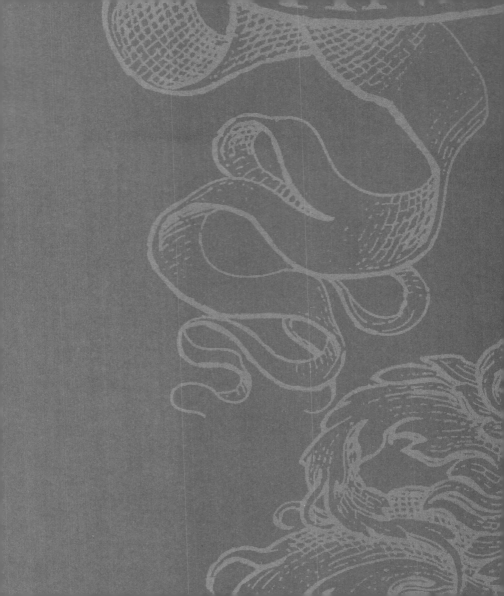

CHAPTER 8

Protection FROM THE Evil Eye OF Envy

The evil eye of envy and jealousy has been described in almost every society throughout the ages. Someone envies your lifestyle, your happiness, your career, your possessions, your children, your home, your vehicles, and your good relationships, and in so doing casts a shadow over them. Indeed, in earlier times it was feared that such a powerful negative gaze could damage or even take away what you love most. In the modern world the concept of the evil eye is not regarded so much as a physical threat, but you may still be adversely affected by feel-bad vibes coming your way from a known or unknown source. Negative energies may be transmitted whenever a resentful person (or people, if you are the target of a whisper-ing campaign in the office or your neighborhood) sees, talks, or thinks negatively about you if you are considered as unfairly fortunate. Such ill-wishing can make you jittery, anxious, irritable, or even unwell, and can jinx you. Therefore, the spells in this chapter are intended to deflect any envy and jealousy, power-ful transmitters of negativity, and to rebound the effects on the sender, thereby protecting you, your loved ones, and all you possess and do.

Don't name the perpetrators in these spells, as to do so weakens the power of the spell.

An All-Purpose Defense
Against the Evil Eye

YOU WILL NEED

A fresh hen's egg in its shell ★ A small clove of garlic

TIMING

*Sunday at dawn, the day and hour of
Michael, archangel of the sun*

THE SPELL

* On the eggshell, invisibly draw an eye with the index finger of your dominant hand.

* Press the egg against the center of your brow, where the evil eye of envy enters. Say, *Eye repel all envy sent, the evil against me now is spent. Return to sender, your power is through. No more am I in thrall to you.*

* Place the egg on a plate and rub the garlic clove all over it, repeating the spell words.

* Boil the egg for 10 minutes, then cast it in water or bury it.

Protection Against the Evil Eye if You Must Live or Work in an Environment Fraught with Jealousy

112

YOU WILL NEED

A blue candle, the traditional color of the protective eye ★ A small sage smudge/incense stick ★ A pot of soil ★ A candle snuffer or a spoon

TIMING

At first light

THE SPELL

* Light the candle and from it the smudge/incense stick, saying, *Eye bright, by day or night. You who envy me, must instantly turn away your eye of jealousy.*

* Turn in all four directions, beginning in the direction directly facing the candle, spiraling the lighted smudge/incense stick, then lower it to the ground and above your head, repeating the spell words for each direction.

* Next, holding the smudge/incense stick like a smoke pen, draw in front of you a large eye shape in the air, level with your brow, repeating the spell words.

* Plunge the smudge/incense into the soil, saying, *The power to stare and glare is done.*

* Extinguish the candle using a snuffer or the back of a spoon.

A Traditional Method to Remove the Evil Eye from Property, People, and Animals

YOU WILL NEED

A small bottle of dark-colored virgin olive oil with a dropper lid ∗ A clear glass bowl of water

TIMING

Sunday at dawn

THE SPELL

∗ Drop olive oil slowly onto the surface of the water, gently turning the bowl until you get an approximate eye shape or circle, even for a moment. It may blur right away, but this is fine.

∗ Swirl the water vigorously in all directions, saying, *Confused, bemused, no longer seen. Cleared from sight, never been.*

∗ Pour the water under a running tap to clear the oil, saying, *The evil eye has flowed away. From all it threatened, safe will stay.*

An Evil Eye Protection Spell
if You Must See the
Perpetrator Regularly

YOU WILL NEED

A blue candle ✳ Any blue crystal or blue glass bead ✳ A
blue candle ✳ A mirror, propped against the wall or another
flat surface, large enough to reflect the candle and your head
and shoulders ✳ Any blue crystal or blue glass bead

TIMING

As darkness falls

THE SPELL

✳ Place the candle in front of the mirror.

✳ Light the candle and stand behind it, so you are reflected in the mirror,
saying, *Reflected away your jealousy, your malice and your enmity.
My eyes send back your own envy.*

✳ Press the crystal against your psychic third eye in the center of your
brow, saying three times, *Three by three, sent back from me, three by three,
returned your envy, transformed to positivity.*

✳ Leave the candle to burn through. Hang the mirror on a wall facing
the front of the house, and suspend the crystal in a cradle or the bead
from a string over the mirror.

Closing the Eye of Evil

YOU WILL NEED

Two large-eyed needles ★ A length of red sewing
thread ★ A bowl of virgin olive oil ★ Scissors

TIMING

After sunset

THE SPELL

* Attach the needles together by knotting the thread.

* Drop the needles into the oil and just above the surface of the oil cut
  the air with the scissors, saying, *Cut is the connection of your jealousy
  to me. My world can you no longer see.*

* Pour away the oil and wash the needles well, hanging them high.

A Second Spell for Closing the Evil Eye if the Attack is Especially Vicious

YOU WILL NEED

A bowl of virgin olive oil ★ A needle

TIMING

During the waning moon and/or Tuesday after sunset

THE SPELL

* Swirl the olive oil, saying, *Look no more with covetous eye on me/my home/my family* [specify the main area of envy]. *I will harm you not, though your envy is damaging me. Close the eye of jealousy, for your hostile sight of me, can no longer be.*

* Gently pierce the oil surface with the sharp end of the needle, repeating the spell words.

* Wrap the needle, still coated in olive oil, in a soft cloth and throw it in the garbage.

To Turn Away the Evil Eye from a Wedding, Christening, or Another Special Occasion if You Know Jealousy is Lurking

YOU WILL NEED

An image of an eye drawn on white paper in soluble blue ink * A bowl of water * A bowl of sand or soil where nothing currently grows

TIMING

The night before the ceremony or event

THE SPELL

* Look down on the eye and say, *You shall not ruin this joyous day. Away with your envy, away I say.*

* Drop the eye image into the water, saying, *Flow and melt away. Your envious eye is washed quite clean, as though it had never been.*

* Once the ink has dissolved, scoop out the paper and bury it in the soil, saying, *The earth as a shield against envy shall be. Joyous shall be this ceremony.*

* Pour the inky water away.

To Prevent a Nasty Neighbor or Relative from Showing Resentment Toward Your New Baby or Small Child

YOU WILL NEED

A stroller ⋆ A chamomile infusion made with a strained chamomile tea bag and boiling water ⋆ Blue beads

TIMING

Before going anywhere you are likely to see the jealous person

THE SPELL

* Surround the stroller with three counterclockwise circles of the cooled infusion, saying, *Resentful eye, come not near. The power of love defeats evil and fear.*

* Hold the beads to your heart, saying, *My maternal/paternal/grandparent protection, enfolds this babe/child from all directions.*

* Attach the beads to the stroller, saying, *The evil eye of envy, turned away, this power shall last by night and day. The beloved child gone from your sight.*

* Throw away the rest of the infusion in the direction in which the person lives.

To Deflect the Covetous Eye of a So-Called Friend or Neighbor Who Flirts with Your Partner

YOU WILL NEED

A blue tiger's eye or a gray agate with an eye formation (very common) ✶ A piece of paper ✶ An elastic band

TIMING

Before a meeting of the three of you

THE SPELL

* Hold the stone between your closed, cupped hands and shake it five times, saying five times, *This is my partner not yours. Out of his/her life get your claws. Your covetous eyes turn away, s/he is mine and mine will stay.*

* Toss the crystal in your open hands, catch it, and close your hands again. Offer the crystal as a gift to the envier and if they refuse, wrap paper around it, secured with an elastic band, and hide it in or as near their home as possible.

To Protect a New Motor Vehicle, Boat, or Precious Item from the Eye of Envy, Cast by Someone Known to You or by Jealous Strangers

YOU WILL NEED

A sandalwood incense stick ∗ A blue bead, if possible
with a black center, or an Eye of Horus charm
(see drawing), the oldest protective eye
charm (dating from ancient Egypt)

TIMING

Just after acquiring the new possession

THE SPELL

∗ Light the incense stick and, using it like a smoke pen, draw smoke
 Eyes of Horus (practice in advance) in the air around the bead or charm,
 first counterclockwise then clockwise, saying, *Look not on*
 [name possession] *covetously. Protect it from all jealousy. Call not
 misfortune down on me, from persons known or envious stranger.
 Guard* [name possession] *from damage and all danger.*

∗ Leave the incense to burn where the smoke will drift over the bead
 or charm.

∗ Hang the bead or charm over the windshield or dashboard, or affix it
 with a small piece of tape to the possession.

If You Suspect Your Business is Being Adversely Affected by Jealous Rivals

YOU WILL NEED

Your business card ∗ Twelve small red jaspers or orange carnelians ∗ A dragon's blood incense stick ∗ A bowl of water

TIMING

Before you open for business

THE SPELL

∗ Surround the business card with the crystals, placing them clockwise around it.

∗ Name each crystal for a different month, starting with the current month, until you have named all twelve crystals, saying also for each crystal, *Every month and every day, the eye of envy is turned away. Now turned back upon itself, returning to me as success and wealth.*

∗ Light the incense stick and draw a huge smoke eye with a cross over it, in the center of the crystals.

∗ Plunge the lighted end of the incense stick into the water. With the wet end, draw an eye on the reverse of the business card and cross it out.

∗ Place the crystals around the premises at regular intervals and, when dry, pin the business card, name outermost, on a wall.

CHAPTER 9

Creating Psychic Wards
AND Wardens
FOR Powerful
Protection

In earlier chapters, I included spells for psychic wards, the invisible psychic exclusion zone magically created around people, places, and possessions. By setting the power within a tangible warden or guardian—a specially empowered object, plant, crystal, or magical symbol—you may reinforce that power. Because wards are such an effective way of protecting yourself from all harm, nastiness, and danger, I have suggested here specific spells that will enclose you in safety in any place and situation and can be easily adapted by changing a few spell words for different needs. You can enhance the protection of your ward by regularly strengthening the wardens or guardians. Magical wards cast around you can at least offer some protection and increase your confidence. You can use anything as a warden, empowering it as you set your psychic boundaries. For example, clothing, jewelry, even a painting in your home, on which you can invisibly etch or actually draw on the back, may hold the power through magical symbols from ancient cultures, such as ancient Egypt, or the Viking or Celtic world. Not only do these timeworn symbols contain the power of their own cultures, but they exude the power of practitioners who have used them magically through thecenturies. Such symbols have a fiercely defensive but empowering significance. Finally, you can call on the protection of existing spirit guardians who live on the land on which your home is built.

To Create a Personal Psychic Exclusion Zone Around Yourself as You Work or Travel

YOU WILL NEED

A red permanent marker

TIMING

Friday at sunset

THE SPELL

* Inside both your shoes and on the label of any of your favorite garments draw in red a tiny scarab beetle (see drawing), the ancient Egyptian symbol of fierce protection against all danger. This image also opens the potential of each new day.

* Put on the shoes and one of the garments and stamp around clockwise in a circle, saying, *Beneath my feet crush all, who step maliciously within this sphere of protection. Guarded by my scarab from all directions, defend me from danger high and low. Scarab, as my guardian, make it so.*

* As you go about your days and journeys, you are surrounded by the ward of the scarab.

To Mark a Psychic Exclusion Zone Around Your Home or Workplace if You Have Received Threats Against the Premises or Encountered Some Security Issues

YOU WILL NEED

1 tablespoon dried dill ✶ 1 tablespoon dried rosemary ✶ 1 green tapered candle ✶ 1 tablespoon dried basil pine or cedar fragrance oil ✶ A mortar and pestle or a bowl and spoon ✶ 1 tablespoon unscented baby powder or cornstarch ✶ A few drops of virgin olive oil ✶ A small padded bag

TIMING

After dark

THE SPELL

* By dim candlelight, mix the herbs with a mortar and pestle, saying, *Fiery rosemary, basil, and dill, keep away harm* [name place], *by your strong will.*

* Add the baby powder/cornstarch and mix with one or two drops of oil.

* Put the mixture in the bag.

* Early in the morning, sprinkle a small quantity of the mixture in front of the premises, saying, *Act for me/us as exclusion zone, that none may enter, causing strife or bringing danger, whether known and feared or threatening stranger.*

* Repeat each morning until the mixture is gone.

To Create a Shadow Power
Animal Guardian

YOU WILL NEED

A small model/statue of your chosen power creature,
set on a flat surface * A plain white or light-colored wall
* Three or four small, lighted candles, set along the
wall behind the model animal (experiment to
find the right position to create its wall shadow)

TIMING

In total darkness except for the lighted candles

THE SPELL

* Look at the shadow made on the wall, saying, *I call from the shadows
  my protector of light. Be with me in danger through day and through night.*

* Blow softly on the candles so the shadow creature moves on the wall,
  saying, *Stand warden for me. My guardian be against all danger
  and iniquity.*

* Blow out the candles, and sit in darkness, saying, *You will be
  with me whenever I call. With you by my side I cannot fail or fall.*

* When you are afraid, call your power creature from the shadows.

A Viking Rune Protection Zone to Prevent Unwanted Visitors or Intrusion into Your Home or Workspace

YOU WILL NEED

A piece of white paper ✳ A red pen ✳ A cup containing different-colored pens, including a black one
✳ A small sticky label

TIMING

Thursday

THE SPELL

✳ On the paper with a red pen, draw an ehwaz (a horse symbol [see drawing]), traditionally used for repelling enemies, but in miniature, effective in its more benign role of preventing disruption.

✳ Stick the label on the black pen, saying, *Not to harm, but to deter, when I am busy come not here, with your malicious chatter and intrusion. That I have time for you is mere illusion.*

✳ Keep the black pen in the cup with the others, symbol facing away from the main door. Never use it for writing.

✳ When unwelcome company approaches, set the symbol facing the door, hidden among the others in the cup.

✳ Turn it around again when potential disruption has gone away.

A Celtic Triple Guardian Ward if You Are Suffering from Spite, Gossip, or Malice in Any Situation You Are Unable to Avoid

YOU WILL NEED

White stones, crystals, or shells ✳ A citrine or amber bracelet, necklace, or earrings ✳ Three small white candles ✳ A small red candle

TIMING

At sunrise

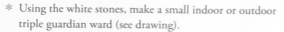

THE SPELL

✳ Using the white stones, make a small indoor or outdoor triple guardian ward (see drawing).

✳ Place the citrine or amber bracelet, necklace, or earrings in the center of the triple guardian ward. This will be your guardian amulet.

✳ Place one white candle at the end of each spiral. (The upper-left coil represents sky/air, the upper right water/sea, and the bottom coil earth.)

✳ Place the red candle, representing fire, in the center of the symbol.

✳ Light each white candle, saying, *The power of three, shall shelter be. Sky, Sea, Earth, and cleansing Fire* [light red candle] *encloses me.*

✳ Blow softly into each white candle, saying, *Three by three, the fourth is Fire. Power enter this amulet and my Guardian be.*

✳ Blow out the white candles.

✳ Leave the red one burning.

✳ Wear your guardian amulet.

A Triple Moon Protective Ward if You Suffer from Nightmares and Night Terrors

YOU WILL NEED

A wooden dream catcher ✳ Olive oil in which
half a teaspoon of powdered vervain (from a
split-open tea bag) has been mixed, gently
heated, and then left to cool

TIMING

The full moon

TRIPLE MOON SYMBOL

THE SPELL

* Put the dreamcatcher flat on a nonporous surface
  and draw the triple moon image in the vervain-infused
  olive oil all around the back of the dreamcatcher hoop, saying,
  *New moon, waxing, full, or wane, I call protection in your name, from
  the terrors of the night. Stand as sister, mother, grandmother until morning
  light. Grandmother Weaver, I call too on you. Be with me this night
  and all year through.*

* When the dreamcatcher is dry, hang it over your bed and anoint
  your inner and outer bedroom door handle with the oil mix.

Celtic Oak Tree Protection Spell
if You Feel Powerless to Stop
Others from Running Your Life

YOU WILL NEED

Red paint ★ A paintbrush or a permanent
marker ★ A strong twig, with the
bark partially scraped off
on one side

TIMING

Thursday

DUIR, THE OAK
SYMBOL

THE SPELL

* Paint or draw the oak tree symbol on the smooth side of the stick,
  saying, *Mighty as the oak, I shall not bow to pressure. My life must
  be my own, my freedom do I treasure. Be for me proud defense,
  let none hurt and dictate. Beneath your sheltering branches,
  I confidently for freedom wait.*

* Stand the oak tree symbol outward in soil in the garden, facing the
  direction from which pressure comes or, if from within the home,
  well hidden in a plant, with the symbol facing where you sit.

Creating a Pentagram Exclusion Zone Against Bullying Because of Your Beliefs by Family Members/People with Whom You Must Live

BANISHING
PENTAGRAM

THE SPELL

* Draw water pentagrams on all the inner doors and windows of your home, picturing the pentagrams as being made of blue light, doubling them in any private space you have, saying, *The enemy is within. Guardian pentagrams, hold fast for me. Around me create, a safe place to wait, where though I survive under difficulty, yet may I be, free to follow my beliefs, with your relief, until my escape.*

* Throw the remaining water outdoors, saying, *Out with anger, prejudice, This is my wish. Protected shall I be, by pentagram power, from this hour.*

If the Threats against or Repression of Your Lifestyle are Coming from Outside the Home, Within the Neighborhood, or from Society in General

YOU WILL NEED

A bowl of salt water, as for the previous spell

TIMING

Just before sunset at the end of the waning moon

THE SPELL

* Draw banishing pentagrams in water on every door and all the windows you can reach on the outside of the house, on outbuildings, external fences, and the outside of gates, saying, *Pentagram power at this hour, none can break through your guard, warden, and warden protector. Stand for me steadfast and hard.*

* Envision pentagrams of blue light shining from every window and door.

* Finally, dip your fingers in the water and draw a banishing pentagram on your brow, saying, *My thoughts are my own. Let none bully me down. By pentagram power, my beliefs shine clear.*

* For both spells, renew the protection each month.

Calling on the Guardians of the Land if Your New Home Has a Troubled History

Four brown candles ✳ Dried lavender or sage, mixed with an equal amount of unsecented baby powder or cornstarch ✳ A new broom ✳ A white candle

Friday at dusk

✳ Place each brown candle on a small table in each inner corner of your home.

✳ Light each brown candle, starting with the one farthest away from the front door and, lighting clockwise, say for each one, *Guardians of this land, sentinel stand. That all shall be well within this home, Guardian, I respectfully entreat you to come.*

✳ Scatter the lavender mix on the front doorstep, then sweep it out, saying, *Old troubles you must now leave, for past sorrows I cannot grieve.*

✳ Place the white candle by an outward-facing window at the front of the house.

✳ Light the white candle, saying, *Guardians of the Land, I guide your way. Enter my home, and as wardens stay.*

✳ Leave the candles to burn and light new ones every Friday evening for at least six weeks.

A Garden Guardian Spell to Deter any Intruders or Misfortune

A large shiny Christmas bauble, disco ball, or ornamental glass fishing float with a hole in the top to which is affixed the hook ★ Fresh sprigs of rosemary

TIMING

Tuesday in the days before the full moon

THE SPELL

* Remove the hook from the bauble and fill the ball with rosemary, saying, *Shine and shimmer like the sun, guardians of the land please come. reflect back with your radiant light, all entering this land/home with malice or with spite. Rosemary of the sun call abundance too.*

* Reattach the hook and hang the bauble from a tree, bush, or even the gutters, saying, *Shimmer and shine, ill fortune and malice be mirrored away. Abundance shall come here, and here shall it stay.*

CHAPTER 10

Protection
FROM Fears,
Phobias, Addictions,
AND Personal
Obsessions

At some point in their lives, many people suffer from phobias or seemingly irrational fears. Among them: obsessive-compulsive disorder or unconsciously overcompensating through excess alcohol consumption or binge-eating and purging—feast and fast.

Some phobias, such as fear of flying or fear of going outdoors, can cripple lives. It is sometimes said that seemingly inexplicable phobias, such as a fear of drowning or a fear of choking, may have their origins in bad experiences in past lives. Self-harming, another symptom of present-world pressure, is distressing, not only for the sufferer but for the sufferer's family.

Gambling, excessive alcohol consumption, or recreational drug use may begin as an anesthetic against life's worries, but can tear families apart. Oftentimes, those who become addicted are led deeper into the addiction by irresponsible friends. Though conventional medical help is and should be the first step in addressing these addictions, spells can play a powerful role in giving strength as the addict takes steps to recovery or works to banish a bad habit.

To Reduce the Effects of Addiction on Other Family Members by Weakening the Power of the Addiction

YOU WILL NEED

A small bar of rose or lavender soap ✳ A bucket of hot water

TIMING

Late evening until the soap disintegrates

THE SPELL

* With the nail on the index finger of your dominant hand, scratch on the soap the name of the addiction and the initials of all family members affected, beginning with the addict.

* Hold the soap and say, *This addiction wounds me/my family grievously. Now I say, its power and destruction shall melt away.*

* Drop the soap in bucket of the hot water (it may take a couple of days to fully disintegrate).

* Add more hot water regularly and pour out the cold water, repeating the spell words.

* When the soap has disintegrated, throw the soapy water down a drain, saying, *Flowing away, this damage to my life/our lives, be gone today.*

* Repeat the spell regularly.

To Reduce the Influence of Drug-Taking Friends or Drug Pushers on Your Teenager or Another Family Member

YOU WILL NEED

Five incense cones ✳ A heatproof dish
✳ Cedar or pine cleanser

TIMING

Begin on Wednesday night, for five consecutive nights

THE SPELL

* Place the incense cones in a heatproof dish, filled with cedar or pine cleanser.

* Light the incense cones rapidly, one after the other, and blow on each tip, saying, *You who profit or encourage through malice this misery, I burn away your contagion, on this and every future occasion. From his/her/my life barred your infectious foulness shall be.*

* When burned through and cool, scatter half the ashes outdoors where they won't blow back, saying, *I cast your evil influences to the winds.*

* Bury the other half deeply, saying, *Ashes to ashes, dust to dust, your evil hold on* [Name], *die it must.*

* Repeat the spell on consecutive nights, reducing the number of incense cones by one each night.

To Overcome a Fear of Flying

Ten small, dark-blue sodalite crystals in a purse

TIMING

Ten days before a trip

THE SPELL

* On the first day, shake the purse, saying, *My life is held back, by my flying fear. Now this outworn panic, no longer comes near.*

* Hide one of the crystals near your home, saying, *I give away my fear. No longer approach or follow me, free shall I be.*

* Each day hide a sodalite farther and farther away from your home.

* On the day of flying, drop the final one in a garbage bin before entering the airport. On takeoff, say, *I gave away my fear. Panic dare no longer come anywhere near.*

To Overcome a Fear of Spiders and Other Crawling Creatures

YOU WILL NEED

Ten very long, thick, dark-colored threads ∗ A small
wooden or wicker hoop (or make one from copper wire)

TIMING

Nine consecutive days

THE SPELL

* On day 1, tie nine knots, starting from the left end along the
  first thread, saying, *I bind my fear of spiders and crawling creatures
  in my life this terror no longer features.*

* Secure both ends tightly to two sides of the hoop, saying,
  I tie up my fear, knotted tight here.

* Do the same for the next eight days until you have created a knot web
  in the hoop.

* Weave the tenth thread around the center of the hoop so it joins all
  the threads in the center in a tangle, saying, *No longer shall I hide.
  In this web my fears are deep inside.*

* Hang the hoop outdoors until the threads disintegrate.

To Overcome an Illogical Fear That Seemingly Comes from a Past Life

YOU WILL NEED

A large natural rock in situ, with a crevice, if possible
* A piece of paper * A green ink pen * A fireproof
pot with sand in the bottom * A small bag

TIMING

Saturday

THE SPELL

* By the large natural rock, write down on the paper
  in green ink your fear, whether of choking, drowning,
  or dying horribly, and over it, to obscure the writing, draw a spiral,
  starting from the inside out (see drawing).

* Burn the paper in the fireproof pot, saying, *I consign this terror to the
  past, set to rest in peace at last, my future free for me to cast.*

* Collect the ashes in a small bag and either push the ashes into the
  crevice or bury them under the stone by moving some earth
  and replacing it.

To Overcome a Bad Gambling Habit, Whether Yours or That of Someone Else in Your Family

YOU WILL NEED

A symbol of gambling, such as betting slips or gambling chips ∗ A small plastic container with a lid

TIMING

Before you or a family member are tempted to gamble

THE SPELL

∗ Hold the betting slip/gambling chips in your closed cupped hands, saying, *Too long have you held me in sway. Too long have I thrown precious money away.*

∗ Fill the container halfway to the top with water and immerse the symbol in it, saying, *I quench the fire, of this destructive desire.*

∗ Put it in the freezer, saying, *Hold on ice, in inaction suspended, temptation ended.*

∗ Whenever tempted, take the container out of the freezer, hold it, and say, *I feel the cold, I feel the ice, suspended, ended.*

∗ When you feel ready, throw the container away, still frozen.

To Reduce Cravings When You
are Giving Up Smoking

YOU WILL NEED

One cigarette ✳ A large bowl of sandalwood or
lavender potpourri ✳ Tea tree or eucalyptus
essential oil ✳ A small, disposable, sealed bag
to carry a little potpourri with you

TIMING

When you have one cigarette left

THE SPELL

* Peel off the cigarette paper and crumble the tobacco into the
potpourri, adding a couple of drops of oil and saying, *Go from me,
craving of intensity.*

* Do this whenever you are tempted at home, wherever you are in
the building or garden.

* If a craving occurs away from home, remove the cigarette paper,
crush the tobacco into the potpourri you are carrying, repeat the spell
words, and throw the bag in the garbage.

* Once a week replace the home potpourri if you have crushed cigarettes
in it, saying the spell words, adding no tobacco, and adding only oil
to the replacement.

When You are Tempted at Home to Have One Too Many Drinks Alone

An open bottle of alcohol

Whenever you are tempted to continue drinking when you are home alone

148

* Before pouring another drink, pour the remaining alcohol in the bottle down the drain under a running cold tap, saying, *Demon drink, down the sink, you befuddle, trouble, muddle me. Water ought you to fix, too much drink and life don't mix.*

* Refill the bottle with water and put on the cap, drinking only that for the rest of the evening.

* Repeat every time you open a bottle of alcohol until you feel ready to put the cap back on after just one or two drinks.

If Social or Business Drinking is a Problem Because You Have Hard-Drinking Friends, Family, or Colleagues

YOU WILL NEED

Dried sharp cloves ★ Half an orange ★ Salt

TIMING

Whenever you feel you might be tempted to drink against your will

THE SPELL

* Press cloves all over the orange flesh to represent the pressures on you to drink excessively, naming cloves for any particular person or situation that causes problems.

* Sprinkle salt on the orange and leave it in a warm place to dry out, saying, *Excessive camaraderie, hard to resist. Yet will I desist. Dry out temptation, with no hesitation, to bring moderation.*

* When the orange has dried out, pull out the cloves, wash and dry them, then carry them in a little pouch during situations where you will be tempted. Gently press a clove in your hand if you're tempted to drink to excess, as a reminder that you are hurting yourself by drinking too much.

If You Have Obsessive-Compulsive Disorder

Seven purple candles * Seven small amethysts
* A purse

TIMING

Seven days, starting on Sunday

THE SPELL

148

* Place the candles in a circle. Place the amethysts in a second circle around the circle of candles.

* Light the candles clockwise, saying, *Burn away this obsession, that will not let me peaceful be. Day by day, from this Sunday, in every way, slow my heart and hands and mind, let me to myself be kind.*

* Pass the first amethyst around the outside of the candle circle, repeating the spell words.

* Extinguish the candles, putting the amethyst in the purse.

* Repeat the spell exactly the same way every day, changing the name of the day.

* On day 7, pass the final amethyst around the candle circle, repeating the spell but leaving the candles to burn through.

* Carry the amethysts with you. When you get a compulsion, hold your amethysts, as many as you need according to the intensity, until the feelings pass.

If You Suffer from Claustrophobia

YOU WILL NEED

A green chrysoprase crystal or any green crystal
on a neck chain * A tall indoor green plant

TIMING

Friday in daylight

THE SPELL

* Go outdoors, holding the crystal where the breeze blows, saying,
  Breath of air, open to me, limitless skies, that all around be.

* Hold the crystal to the light, saying, *Breath of the sun, limitless light,
  open my sight, that I may be free.*

* Take it indoors, hang the crystal on the plant, and sprinkle a few grains
  of soil over it, saying, *Breath of the earth, give my new courage birth.
  Grant space all around me wherever I be.*

* Water the plant, washing the crystal as you do so, saying, *Breath of the
  waters, sea of tranquility, limitless ocean, flows now before me.*

* Whenever you have to be anywhere potentially claustrophobic, wear the
  pendant, and while touching it, call on the limitless sky, sun, waters,
  and earth to open up around you and let you breathe freely.

If You Fear Going Out of the House

A bubble blower * Bubble mix

Beginning of the waxing moon

* Indoors, open a downstairs window and blow bubbles through it, saying, *Free as a bird, you rise through the skies, free to go anywhere, so can I.*

* Next time, when you are ready, open the front door and blow bubbles from inside the door outward, repeating the spell words.

* The next stage is to stand outside the door, blowing bubbles toward the street, saying the same spell words.

* Continue taking small steps until you are ready to go to the end of the street, where you can purse your lips, blow imaginary bubbles, and say the spell words to give yourself confidence.

If You Suffer from an Eating Disorder

YOU WILL NEED

Chamomile or lavender pure essential oil ★ Apricot oil
(optional) ★ A small container with a screw-top lid

TIMING

Whenever you feel out of control

THE SPELL

* Stop and gently massage your hands and feet with the chamomile or lavender oil, if you wish diluted in three times the quantity of apricot oil, saying as a mantra, *My body is my temple, within it my lovely soul. I treat myself with gentleness, I am beautiful and whole.*

* Add the mix to your bath or place it on a washcloth in a shower, saying the spell words again.

* Carry a small quantity of the oil with you in a sealed container.

* Whenever you feel you must treat your body harshly to fit an impossible ideal, take out the oil you can carry with you and gently anoint the center of your brow, the base of your throat, and your inner wrist points, repeating the spell words in your mind.

If You Need to Lose Weight, But Always Fail

A blue pen ⋆ A piece of paper ⋆ A green
bag or purse ⋆ Nine hazelnuts

TIMING

Before you start a new diet

THE SPELL

* With a blue pen, write on the paper an aim you can achieve now.
  Fold the paper small, putting it in the bag with the hazelnuts.

* Shake the closed bag nine times, saying, *I will healthier be,*
  my body weight in harmony. No more famine and no more feast,
  but enjoying all I moderately eat.

* Each morning state your current and future goals, and shake the bag
  nine times while repeating the spell words.

* When you are tempted to binge, shake the bag nine times, repeating
  the spell words in your mind or out loud.

* Every nine days, replace the nuts, repeating the whole spell and,
  when necessary, revising your goals as you move closer to achieving
  them. At that point, write in blue on the other side of the paper an aim
  now that you feel you are in better shape.

If You are a Shopaholic

YOU WILL NEED

Unwanted purchases in a bag(s) to sell or give to charity

TIMING

When you realize you are overspending

THE SPELL

* When the bag(s) are packed, say, *Enough for my needs and a little more, not emptying every department store. Pleasure in buying but not overspending, my stockpiling and hoarding now shall be ended.*

* Dispose of the unwanted items after taking a screenshot of the stockpile on your phone.

* When you are tempted to binge-spend before buying, call up the photo on your mobile device and repeat the spell words.

If You or a Loved One Self-Harms

*Note: Adapt the words if a loved one is in danger
of hurting themselves.*

YOU WILL NEED

A bowl of loose pearls ★ A soft pink velvet drawstring bag

TIMING

If you feel the urge to hurt yourself

THE SPELL

* Run your fingers through the bowl of pearls and then hold the bowl,
  blowing gently into it, afterwards saying, *Though I despair, for myself
  I will care, not harm. I reach out for calm.*

* Select a pearl and place it in the bag, closing the bag and saying,
  *I am of worth, to walk in beauty on the earth. I shut up the pain,
  and become complete again.*

* Repeat the spell each time you feel the pain rising and, when the bag is
  full, have the pearls strung on a necklace and wear it to remind yourself
  of your immense value.

To Protect a Loved One/Child Whose Eccentric or Antisocial Behavior Stems from a Psychological or Medical Condition

YOU WILL NEED

A small pink modeling clay figure of your loved one/child
* Small rose quartz crystals or pink glass nuggets
* A circle of six pink candles * A pastel silk scarf

TIMING

The night before going somewhere challenging

THE SPELL

* Into the modeling clay figure of your loved one/child, press the rose quartz crystals.

* Place the figure into the circle of pink candles.

* Light each candle clockwise, saying for each one, *Enclose my loved one/ child in kindness, that love to and from him/her will shine. Keep away all who mock, are shocked, or complain. I ask no more for this loved one of mine, nor less, than that his/her beautiful inner soul, may not radiate in vain.*

* Leave the candles to burn through, then wrap the figure in the silk scarf, knotting it and saying, *Safe within my love.*

* Keep the wrapped figure with your special possessions, replacing it and redoing the spell when the figure crumbles.

If You Exercise Excessively to the Detriment of Your Health, Your Life, and Your Relationships

Note: This also works for workaholics, modifying the words.

YOU WILL NEED

A white candle ★ Meditation music (instrumental; no lyrics)

TIMING

When you would normally be exercising

THE SPELL

* Create a comfortable place where you can sit and gaze into a lighted candle, playing soft music.

* Set your timing device for 5 minutes and do nothing, except breathe gently, no matter how hard it is at first not to be pushing your body.

* When you have finished, blow out the candle, saying, *Enough is enough, not exercising is tough. Yet there must be balance, shall there be rest, activity is fine, but not to excess.*

* Each day try to increase your quiet time by 5 minutes until you can sit meditating/relaxing without needing to time yourself.

If You Suffer from Panic Attacks

A crystal with a hole in the middle, called a doughnut
stone, in pink rose quartz or turquoise

TIMING

A calm, clear day

THE SPELL

* Hold the crystal to your lips and slowly and gently breathe through
  the hole, saying afterward, *Calm flows from me and toward me,
  I embrace tranquility. Nothing shall henceforward panic me.*

* Touch the crystal, saying, *Henceforward, you are my token of harmony,
  wherever I may be.*

* Keep the stone attached to your keys or an item you always have with
  you. When you are in a situation where you feel panic rising, feel for the
  hole in the crystal center, and breathe slowly while repeating the spell
  words in your mind as a mantra.

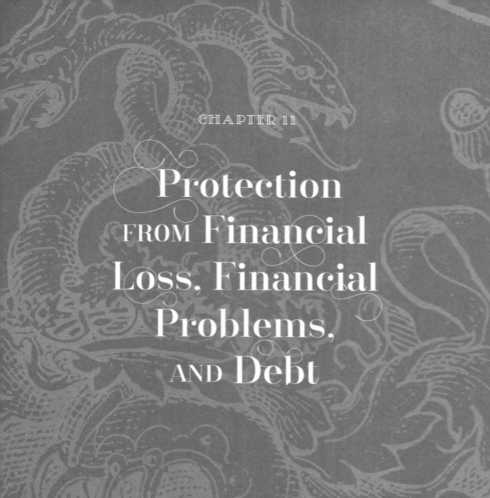

CHAPTER 11

Protection FROM Financial Loss, Financial Problems, AND Debt

Financial worries are one of the main reasons people turn to spells, especially if they are being harassed by creditors or find that they simply can't meet their financial obligations. At times, official channels and charities can help, and sometimes unexplored ways of making money can be found. You might also be able to figure out new ways to economize. But some creditors can be ruthless, even while just keeping within the law. And with spiraling interest rates on unpaid debts and offers from unscrupulous lenders, it is hard not to get into even deeper trouble. Pension funds may lose value or businesses may be affected by global downturns, leaving an individual or a small company seemingly at the hands of fate. Likewise, those who do not pay what is owed to a one-person or small business, reliant on regular inflow, can knock a viable venture totally off course. Above all, money can be used as a weapon by unscrupulous exes, while those we love can sometimes use that love and accompanying responsibility we feel to get a free financial ride.

It is hard to focus on anything with such 24/7 pressure. However, spells can help to generate abundance, give impetus to struggling businesses, repel threats from the unscrupulous, and sometimes open unexpected doors to new opportunities to make more money or access a helpful new way to ease financial problems.

To Gradually Reduce Debt

A long thin piece of white paper ✳ A purple pen ✳ A fast-burning, dark-blue or purple candle ✳ A lidded pot

TIMING

Saturday

THE SPELL

* On the paper, top to bottom in seven equal-sized rectangles, write in purple—largest at the top and gradually descending in size to the bottom—DEBT BE REDUCED TO SIZE.

* Light the candle, saying, *May my debts be reduced to size.*

* Tear off the top rectangle of paper and rip it into small pieces, dropping the pieces into the pot and saying, *Now my debts are cut down to size.*

* Repeat the words and actions until all the ripped-up rectangles are in the pot. Put on the lid and seal it with melted candle wax, saying, *Contained and restrained.*

* Extinguish the candle, throw it away, and keep the sealed pot near the final letters of demand or next to your computer, if the demands are in your email inbox.

To Find Helpful Official Support if Unscrupulous Creditors are Pressuring You

YOU WILL NEED

A purple candle ★ Financial papers ★ Dried tarragon, the dragon's herb, in a small dish

TIMING

Wednesday

THE SPELL

* Light the candle, saying, *Illumine the path to those who will help me find the way, that my finances will become secure again and in stability stay.*

* Hold the papers up to the candlelight, repeating the spell words.

* Hold the dish with tarragon toward the light, saying, *Guide me to the right source, to take away force and manipulation. And act decisively on my behalf, without hesitation.*

* Scatter the tarragon outside the front door, in all four directions, as you turn clockwise, saying, *Winds of the north, east, south and west, guide me to whoever can help me best.*

* Leave the candle to burn while you do online research for the right help.

If Money Flows Out of Your Life Faster Than it Flows in

YOU WILL NEED

A jug ✳ A lidded plastic container ✳ A saucepan

TIMING

Near the full moon, ongoing

THE SPELL

* Half-fill the jug, saying, *Flowing in, staying here, inflow not outflow, money must not go. That much is clear.*

* Pour the water from the jug into the plastic container and freeze it, saying, *going nowhere, held on ice, saving for a rainy day. Now won't that be nice.*

* Gently melt the ice with a little extra water in the saucepan until steam rises, saying, *Expanding, spreading, money no more shall I be shedding.*

* Leave it to cool and say, *Profit and gain, no more money down the drain.*

* Pour the cooled water on thriving plants.

If Your Money-Making Ventures Have Hit an Impasse or Downturn

A lidded pot of sunflower seeds

On a full moon night

* Shake the pot seven times, saying, *Stagnant, stuck, I'll soon change this luck. Expanding again, reversing the drain.*

* Leave the uncovered pot of seeds outdoors all night to absorb the full moonlight.

* In the morning, scatter some of the seeds to the winds, saying, *I spread my resources far and wide, not waiting or cowering afraid inside.*

* Bury some of the seeds, saying, *Slower growth shall follow through, I will take steps and rebuild anew.*

* Cast the remaining seeds into flowing water, saying, *Taking a chance, on an unlikely win, I call on the waters, send prosperity in.*

If a Substantial Payment Owed to You is Long Overdue and the Situation is Hurting You Financially

YOU WILL NEED

A small, open glass jar * Seven green currency notes
of any value or seven gold-colored coins * Dried basil

TIMING

Seven days, initially

THE SPELL

* Shake the jar and say, *An empty pot, not a lot. You* [name debtors large and small], *You're not paying and so I'm saying, pay now, I don't care how, about your sick cat, or your trip to the moon. Just pay up in full—and soon.*

* Put a note or a coin in the jar with a sprinkling of basil, the fierce money herb, and shake the jar, saying, *Starting today, you swiftly must pay.*

* Continue for seven days, then send a serious demand, threatening action and/or bad publicity.

A Send-Money-Fast Spell When You are Desperately in Need of the Money

A Chinese money candle with a coin in it or a
slightly melted beeswax candle in which you have
pushed a coin or a quartz crystal down low
★ A bowl of salt ★ A thin-bladed knife

TIMING

*When there is no time or opportunity to
seek resources conventionally*

166

THE SPELL

* Touch the coin in the candle five times, light the candle, and sprinkle
a little salt in the flame, saying faster and faster, *Candle shine,
money glow, the wolf is at the door, you know. Send the money I urgently
need* [specify as precisely as possible to the last cent]. *This is an
emergency indeed.*

* Blow out the candle, relight it, and burn it until the coin falls out,
pouring the rest of salt under a running tap.

* In the warm melted wax, press the coin and write the required amount
and NEEDED URGENTLY in it with the knife.

If You Urgently Need to Economize

YOU WILL NEED

A small, beeswax candle ∗ A piece of paper, with
EXTRAVAGANCE written in red on one side and
ECONOMY written in brown on the other
∗ A deep fireproof pot half-filled with sand
or soil ∗ A small, edible luxury item ∗ A silver-
colored coin on a plate close to the candle

TIMING

Whenever you are tempted to spend money excessively

THE SPELL

∗ Light the candle, saying, *Living in luxury, Can no longer be. Saving for a rainy day, shall be my new everyday way.*

∗ Tear off a corner of the paper, burning it in the candle and dropping it in the pot, saying, *Economy will set me free, to provide daily necessity.*

∗ Eat the luxury item, saying, *Indulging occasionally, must be sufficient now for me.*

∗ When the coin is coated with wax, ease it out, and when it cools, keep it near where you keep your receipts.

∗ Continue the spell weekly until you have a set of wax-coated coins and the paper is entirely burned.

If You Know a Close Relative or Friend is Stealing from You

A modeling clay figure with extra-long arms
★ Blue twine or string ★ A blue cloth

TIMING

Thursday evening

THE SPELL

* Fold the clay figure's arms so they are behind its back and secure them with twine, saying, *Keep your thieving hands off what is mine, at stealing from a friend/relative I draw the line. I bind you from stealing and trickery, only when you desist will I set you free.*

* Keep the figure in a drawer wrapped in blue cloth near the location from which things or money disappear.

If You are Facing Bankruptcy or are Under Threat of Having Your Assets Seized

YOU WILL NEED

A box of metal paper clips ✳ A copy of a final demand
✳ A fireproof pot, half-filled with sand or soil

TIMING

Whenever the need is dire

THE SPELL

✳ Place paper clips all around the edges of the demand, saying, *Though assaulted I am on every side, and there seems nowhere to hide, time I need, Space to breathe. Yet I believe, I will not go down. Even under threat, I shall not drown.*

✳ Remove the paper clips from the paper and set fire to paper in the pot outdoors, saying, *One last chance before I fall, cosmos, angels, human aid, help me as I call. Courage and power come alive, I can fight on, I will survive.*

✳ Make the paper clips into lucky horseshoes and make one last-ditch attempt at negotiation.

If Your Business or Financial Viability is Being Adversely Affected by a Dismal Economy

YOU WILL NEED

Ten green twigs ∗ A tidal river, the ocean on the outflowing tide, or fast-flowing water ∗ Ten yellow flowers ∗ A packet of poppy or sunflower seeds in a basket

TIMING

Sunday morning, during the waxing moon

THE SPELL

∗ Begin by casting the ten twigs, one after the other, into the water, saying, *Tide turn, prosperity return. I trust in inevitability, that better times I shall see.*

∗ Repeat with the flowers.

∗ Plant or scatter the seeds on the banks of the river or on the soil nearest the ocean, saying, *I will survive, once again shall I thrive. The tide is turning, prosperity returning. Until then I will strive to turn loss into gain, and so my fortunes can turn again.*

∗ Go home and create a master plan for taking advantage of the downturn in the current economic climate to prosper.

If You Fear Someone Close is About to Engage in a Get-Rich-Quick Scheme That Appears Certain to Be a Scam

YOU WILL NEED

A pile of money, any denomination
* Nine small red candles * A dish

TIMING

Sunday at noon

THE SPELL

* Put your hands around the money, saying, [Name], *you tell me that this scheme is safe, that your money can't possibly escape. Yet it seems this is delusion and quick money-making pure illusion.*

* Knock down the pile and then push the money into another pile, so you can enclose it in a circle of the red candles.

* Light the candles clockwise, saying, *I earmark your money, this is a scam, someone else's bread and jam. Listen to me, before your finances become history.*

* Leave the candles to burn and put the money on an open dish in a warm place.

* Come up with alternative money-making strategies, based on facts and figures.

If You Have a Chance to Make Big Money, But Know There is Risk Involved

YOU WILL NEED
Three dice

TIMING
Wednesday

THE SPELL

* Shake all the dice three times in your open cupped hand, saying,
  A time to win, not to lose, I know which option I shall choose.
  To take a chance and to win through, Dame Fortune, this I ask of you.

* Now do the same with two dice, saying, *Roll the dice for me,*
  Dame Fortune, bringing rich rewards and soon. Protect me in this
  speculation, so I don't bust but boom.

* Roll just one dice, saying, *Lady Luck, don't hesitate, guard me as*
  I speculate, and bring me fortune on a plate.

* Carry the dice with you and shake all three before taking a chance.

If Your Ex-Partner is Using the Children to Blackmail You Financially

YOU WILL NEED

Three or four money herbs, such as dried basil, bay leaves, chamomile, marjoram, oregano, sage, thyme, or vervain ★ A red bag ★ A bowl and spoon ★ A lighted beeswax candle on a flat metal base ★ Lavender potpourri

TIMING

Before contact or a visit

THE SPELL

* Mix the herbs in the red bag, saying louder and faster, *you blackmail and tether me, unless with everything I agree. I have had enough. I call your bluff.*

* End with a final bang of the spoon in the bowl on the final *bluff.*

* Shake the closed bag, repeating the spell words.

* Scatter the herbs from the bag into the melting wax, saying, *Your pressures on the family, now shall restricted be. For your blackmail is bound, as are you. Totally, your threats are through.*

* Throw away the herbs and wax, putting lavender potpourri in the bag.

If Aging Parents are Dangling the Prospect of Inheritance in Order to Control You

YOU WILL NEED

A blue figure out of modeling clay, representing you ⋆ A box with a lid and a key ⋆ Old coins or currency ⋆ Brown modeling clay figures, representing your parents

TIMING

Next time you give in to pressure

THE SPELL

※ Put the figure of yourself in the box pressed under the money and lock it, saying, *You lock me up with promises, you take away the key. Control me with inheritance one day mine, if a good girl/boy I be.*

※ Remove your figure from the box and reroll it into a ball, burying it under a thriving tree or basil plant, saying, *Henceforth I grow in my own way, bound no more by promises of a future day. Either give me the money willingly, when right to be, or leave me free.*

※ Put the parent figures in the box with their money and lock it.

If Disastrous Investments or Personal Problems Have Left You Without Money or Prospects

YOU WILL NEED

Children's toy bricks, formed into a tower

TIMING

The beginning of a week or month

THE SPELL

* Knock down the tower, saying, *Without foundations all collapsed, my claim to fortune truly lapsed. Yet shall I rebuild again, turn wisdom learned by loss to gain.*

* Build carefully with the toy bricks a wall with a firm base, adding extra bricks that were not in the tower, and say, *No recriminations, no procrastination, but step by step and brick by brick, finances will grow and this time stick.*

* Take a picture of the wall on your smartphone or another device as a reminder and give the toy bricks to a child.

If Your Family or Friends are Bleeding You Dry Financially

A flat black stone ∗ A candle small enough
to stand on top of the stone

TIMING

After one too many demands

THE SPELL

∗ Place your hands around the stone and say, *Blood out of a stone you*
[name the worst financial parasites], *leave me alone. You bleed me dry
with your poverty cry.*

∗ Light the candle on top of the stone, saying, *No more your source of extra
income, no longer are your demands welcome. This light is for me and me
alone. This is my guardian stone. Protect against sob stories and major guilt
trips, you and I no longer financially are joined hip to hip.*

∗ Keep the stone inside next to the front door. When you're expecting a
visit or you receive mailed appeals, light the candle on the stone,
and say the spell words.

If People at Your Workplace are Engaged in Dishonest Financial Dealings in Which You are Being Unfairly Implicated

YOU WILL NEED

A red pen ✳ Paper ✳ Dried lemongrass or sprigs of lemongrass ✳ A blank envelope

TIMING

Wednesday before work

THE SPELL

* With a red pen, write on the paper the names of all those who are trying to falsely implicate you in their scheme.

* Sprinkle lemongrass over the paper, saying, *Protect me from these human snakes, that they will make enough mistakes. So caught will be in their dishonesty, without in the slightest implicating me.*

* Shred or cut the paper into tiny pieces, put it in a blank envelope, seal the envelope, and dump it in the garbage bin nearest to where you work.

* Repeat the spell every Wednesday, using ever smaller paper and writing smaller until you can write no more. On the last Wednesday, put a tiny piece of blank paper in the envelope having said the spell words over it five times.

If You Are Living on a Fixed Income or Pension and Hate Being Poor

Nothing

Beginning at early morning light, if possible in sunshine

* Stand in the morning light with your arms extended high and wide, saying, *I welcome the dawning of the morning, I greet infinite possibility. I can still learn, so I can more earn, use my ingenuity financially.*

* Repeat the spell words and actions at noon and again at sunset, saying at sunset, *This is not the sunset if my life, no way. I will develop each new day, growing success. I will not settle for less.*

* Take up a former interest that, if developed, could make money; study something new; or start a small business venture.

If You Have a Major Tax Dispute or Have Received an Unfair Official Financial Demand

YOU WILL NEED

A piece of paper on which you have written the name of the tax officer or department making the demand ★ A dark glass jar with a lid ★ Uncooked rice or flax seeds to represent financial security ★ Nine small iron pyrites ★ Two crushed dragon's blood or frankincense incense cones ★ Sealing wax or tape

TIMING

When you are in dispute

THE SPELL

* Fold up the paper until it's small and put it in the bottom of the jar, followed by the rice, the pyrites pushed into the rice, and, finally the incense, saying, *I have given much, yet they demand more. Keep the IRS from my door.*

* Secure the jar top very firmly with sealing wax or layers of tape, and put it upside down in your home workspace, saying, *Topsy turvy, leave me alone. Your power to hassle me, Is turned upside down.*

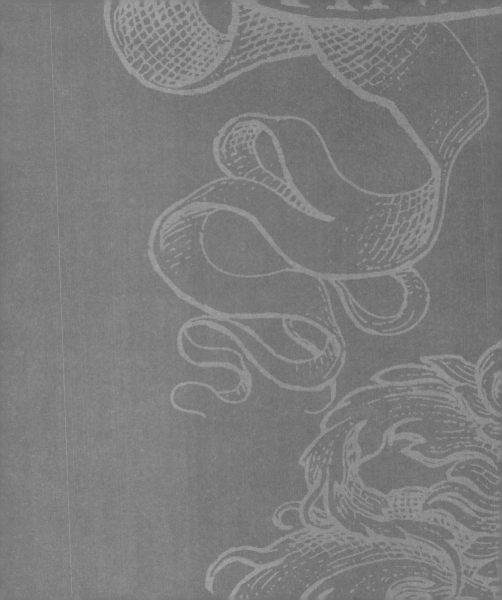

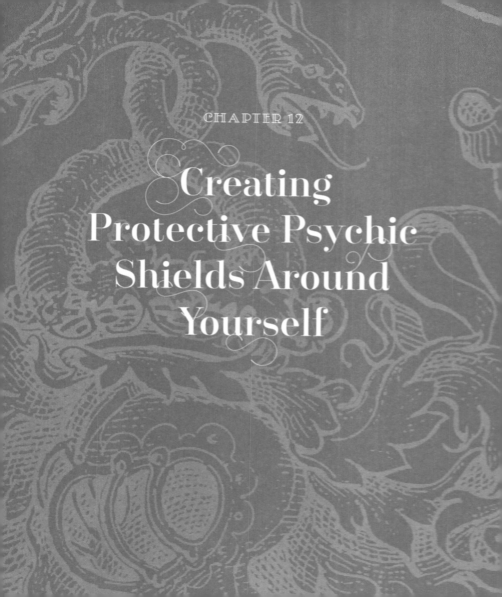

CHAPTER 12

Creating Protective Psychic Shields Around Yourself

Psychic shields are similar to psychic wards, but more versatile. A psychic shield is a personal protective device that, once set up, can be activated at any time and in any place when the need arises. You can, of course, adapt any of the following spells to protect loved ones by naming them and sending a shield around them. For example, you can cast the Archangel Samael Shield of Fire if you have a family member in the armed forces or the Archangel Camael Shield for a teenager being bullied.

You can reactivate these at the beginning of each week, using the suggested trigger symbols I have listed for each shield. The following spells initially activate the energies of the chosen shield and, once created, it remains in the background until you call upon it. In practice, you will find the shield coming around you spontaneously in your time of need. Though I have suggested shields for many different needs, you will find that three or four shields will offer protection for most of your needs and lifestyle. For example, the All-Purpose Archangel Michael Light Shield, or the Shield of your Guardian Angels and Spirit Guides, or Archangel Raziel's Shield of Invisibility, when you need to suddenly lower your profile, whether in a potentially confrontational situation at work or if you are traveling alone at night and you encounter drunks or threatening crowds, or when you are in total isolation.

A Michael, Archangel of the Sun, All-Purpose Shield Against All Harm and Danger

YOU WILL NEED

Six gold candles, set in a semicircle ✳ A mirror propped against a wall, so you can see the candles in it and your head and shoulders as you stand behind them

TIMING

Sunday night in darkness

THE SPELL

* Light the candles, so there is a halo of light around you as you stand behind them.

* Say, *Shield of gold, around me unfold, this Michael light, of dazzling might.*

* Raise your arms above your head, at extended arm's length, moving them down, still extended, around your shoulders, and say, *Michael, be my Shield, and never yield.*

* Shake your hands in front of you, still looking in the mirror.

* Extend your arms again over your head and around your shoulders, picturing a golden force field of sparks around your energy field.

* Blow out the candles.

* To activate the shield, shake your hands in front of you.

A Cassiel, Archangel of Stillness, Shield to Restore Calm and Balance if You or Others Are Panicking

Four purple candles ✳ An amethyst on a table
✳ Four myrrh or musk incense cones on a heatproof plate

TIMING

Whenever you or others are panicking

THE SPELL

184

✳ Set the four candles in a square around the amethyst.

✳ Light the candles clockwise and light one incense cone from each of
them, saying, *Cassiel, spread your shield of tranquility, all around me.
That whenever I panic or others are losing control, your Shield will soothe
my heart and soul.*

✳ Place the incense outside the candle square and, with your hands, gently
waft the smoke toward the amethyst, repeating the spell words softly
and slowly until they fade in silence.

✳ Leave the candles and incense to burn through.

✳ Carry your amethyst whenever you know people will be rushing around
like headless chickens, and breathe gently into it to activate the shield.

An Archangel Raphael Shield to Protect Against Spite, Lies, and Human Snakes

YOU WILL NEED

A sparkling yellow citrine

TIMING

Before noon

THE SPELL

* Leave the citrine in morning light from dawn to almost noon.

* Then gently press the citrine against your solar plexus energy center, your inner sun, situated in the center of the top of your stomach, saying, *Raphael, With inner sunshine, make this shield, that to human snakes I do not yield. Protect me against those who spread lies and spite. Drive them back with your dazzling light.*

* When you know an attack is imminent, gently press your solar plexus with the index finger of your dominant hand or with the citrine and say the spell words in your mind to activate the shield.

An Archangel Camael Shield
to Give Strength and Courage to
Overcome Anger and Persecution

A red candle ★ A red jasper or garnet

TIMING

Tuesday, the day of Camael

THE SPELL

* Light the candle and begin tossing the crystal higher and faster, saying nine times, *Red of strength, red of courage, camael shield me from persecution and rage. With your iron shield me enclose, that none may weakness in me expose.*

* Catch the crystal and blow out the candle, scattering the red light around you.

* To activate the shield, gently shake anything red between your hands if you do not have the crystal with you.

The Asmodel Shield of Pink to Protect You Against Those Who Emotionally Manipulate You Through Guilt or False Love

YOU WILL NEED

A rose quartz crystal ✶ Fresh pink rose petals or rose potpourri in a bowl

TIMING

Friday

THE SPELL

✶ Add the rose quartz to the rose petals and gently run your hands through them, saying, *Asmodel, set your shield of self-love around me, to protect against those who manipulate me, through vulnerability. Let me be kind, but clear of mind, And of their web of guilt be free.*

✶ Replace the petals regularly or use rose potpourri.

✶ Whenever you know you are going to see the manipulative person, run your hands through the bowl and repeat the spell words to activate the shield or carry the crystal with a few rose petals in a purse.

The Archangel Sachiel Shield to Protect You Against Injustice and False Accusations

YOU WILL NEED

A small aquamarine or a clear quartz crystal
★ A small, blue, wide-necked glass lidded bottle

TIMING

Thursday

THE SPELL

* Put the crystal in the bottle, add water, and put on the lid, shaking the bottle three times and saying, *Wise Sachiel, surround me with your shield of blue, that it may be believed what I say is true. Lies and injustice drive away, and my accusers unmasked in the light of your day.*

* After 24 hours, splash the water in the center of your hairline, the center of your brow, the base of your throat, and each inner wrist point to shield your higher energy centers that are being attacked.

* Keep the bottle refilled and carry it to activate the Sachiel shield by anointing yourself whenever you are under attack.

The Shield of Your Guardian Angels and Spirit Guides to Be with You Day and Night

YOU WILL NEED

Two large white feathers

TIMING

Early Sunday

THE SPELL

* Go to a high, open space and spiral the feathers all around you as you turn six times clockwise, crossing and uncrossing the feathers, holding them an extended arm span in front of you. Say, *Guardian angels and guides, may the shield of your wings offer sanctuary, that each day protected I shall be. From all fears and hazards large and small. Keep me safe when I do call.*

* Leave one feather to be blown away and keep the other near a window to touch each morning and evening to activate your 24/7 shield.

The Shield of Your Power Animals to Protect You in Lonely and Hazardous Places

YOU WILL NEED

A flashlight ★ Plan in your mind (or you may already know) the species to fly above you, one to walk on either side of you (the same species), and one that stays close to the earth or lives under it that moves close to your feet, watching for danger

TIMING

Around sunset

THE SPELL

* Switch on the flashlight and, turning slowly and continuously clockwise, call each of your creatures, shining the flashlight above you, on either side of you, and toward your feet. Say, as a soft chant, *You who fiercely guard and fly, on the ground or soaring high. Round me draw close, in hazardous places and when alone and I fear the most.*

* Looking straight ahead, switch the flashlight beam on and off and walk home before dark.

* Call their names whenever you are afraid.

The Mirror Shield to Reflect Back Curses, Hexes, Jinxes, and the Evil Eye

YOU WILL NEED

Four mirrors—one facing you, one behind you, and one on either side of you, angled so you can see yourself from all directions, at least head and shoulders

TIMING

In sunlight

THE SPELL

* Raise your arms upward, forming an arch around your head, and then out at your sides, then extend both hands in an arch in front of you toward the ground, saying, *On all four sides, up and down, the mirror shield shall me surround. Reflecting back negativity, from earthly source or paranormally, three times rebounds.*

* Carry a small mirror with you that you can direct toward any malevolence to activate the shield.

The Archangel Samael Shield of Fire to Protect You Against Physical Danger and Attack

Note: This is also good if you have a family member
on active service in a war zone.

Nine red candles, placed around the room, so
you can safely stand in the middle of the room, or
make the candle circle on a table and face it

TIMING

Tuesday after dark

THE SPELL

* Light the candles clockwise, saying for each one, *Within this shield of Samael fire, no physical danger can transpire. Though I may face fierce attack, your fiery protection I shall not lack. I shall be safe, I shall not yield, guarded by my Samael shield.*

* Blow out the candles fast, counterclockwise, saying, *Flame and flare, Samael be there.*

* Before you or a loved one enters a place of danger, light a red candle or picture one in your mind, activating the shield.

The Archangel Gabriel Shield of the Moon to Protect You and Your Unborn Child During Pregnancy and Delivery

YOU WILL NEED

A moonstone or clear crystal sphere ★ A glass or crystal bowl of water ★ Small white flowers, such as jasmine, the moon flower

TIMING

The first full moon after conception

THE SPELL

* Place the crystal in the bowl of water outdoors, on the ground, scattering flowers around the outside of the bowl.

* Sit under the moon or moon power, if it is cloudy.

* Dip your hands in the water, saying, *Mother Moon, on this your night, I take in your silvery shield of light. Calling on Gabriel, to add his power, to surround my babe at every hour, until in my arms my child I hold. In moonlight and on moon wings, I ask you enfold.*

* Filter the water into bottles.

* To strengthen the shield anytime, anoint your/your partner's womb.

The Archangel Azrael Shield of Valor to Guard You Against All Fear, Whether Within You or Caused by Others

YOU WILL NEED

A miniature ornamental sword or a silver- or gold-colored letter opener

TIMING

Tuesday

THE SPELL

* With the blade, gently touch your brow, your left and right shoulders, then your navel, your left and right knee, and, finally, your left and right foot, saying for each one, *Azrael, give me valor with your sword, and hold high your shield. That all fear, however caused, will fade and disappear.*

* Finally, thrust the sword outward, saying, *Begone all fears. My shield of valor does appear.*

* To activate the Azrael shield, use anything pointed, extended outward in front of you, even a key or a pen, saying in your mind, *Begone all fears. My shield of valor does appear.*

The Archangel Raziel Shield of Invisibility for Keeping a Low Profile

YOU WILL NEED

A sagebrush smudge stick ⁕ A pot of soil

TIMING

Outdoors on a misty day

THE SPELL

⁕ Light the smudge stick and gently and rhythmically spiral it, chanting softly and slowly over and over again, *Raziel, with your shield of invisibility, hide me within mists that none may see. My presence, not even my essence, unnoticed shall I be.*

⁕ Extinguish the smudge stick by plunging it, lighted end down, into the pot of soil. Alternatively, you could bury it deep in the earth, where it will instantly be extinguished.

⁕ Blow gently through your mouth to activate the Raziel shield.

The Jophiel Sunshine Shield if You Are Surrounded by Negative or Critical People

YOU WILL NEED

A suncatcher crystal on a chain or a clear quartz pendulum ⋆ A glass bowl of water set in bright sunlight

TIMING

In bright sunshine or, if it's not sunny, use a semicircle of lighted yellow candles

THE SPELL

* Plunge the suncatcher into the water, saying, *Sunbeams of Jophiel shimmer around me, to create my shield of positivity. That none will bring me down, discourage or depress, stress or cause undue duress. Surround me with sunlight every day, whether skies be blue or clouded with gray.*

* Scatter a few drops of the sun-water on yourself, filtering the rest to splash on pulse points when you're discouraged by others.

* Hang the pendulum or suncatcher at home or at work, and spiral it to activate the shield.

The Archangel Remiel Shield of the Storms to Guard You Against Troublemakers

A meteorite or a piece of lava (even a bit of pumice stone)

*A stormy day when you can see lightning
and hear thunder in the distance*

* Stand outdoors and lift your hands high, close to your head, fists clenched, holding the meteorite in your dominant hand and say, *I am the rain, and the rain empowers me to resist those who make trouble and mischief in my life. An end of your trouble and strife, for I call down the storm-filled shield of Remiel. Guard me well.*

* Repeat the spell words and movements, substituting the word *thunder* for *rain.*

* Then substitute *lightning* for *rain*, and, finally, *storm.*

* Go indoors and watch the storm. Hold your meteorite in your clenched fist to activate the Remiel shield.

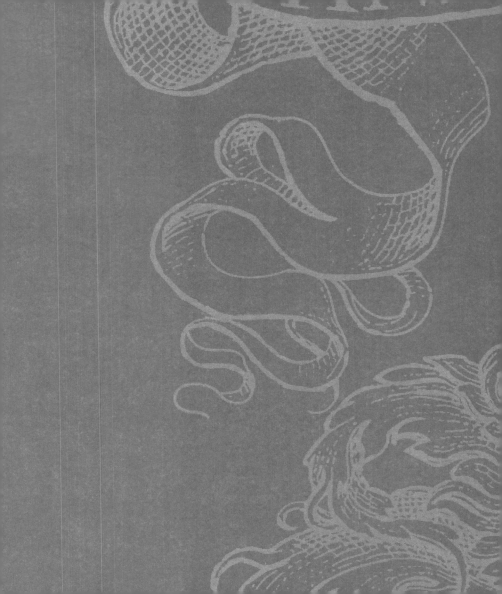

CHAPTER 13

Protection of the Home and All Within

Home is precious, whether it's a room in a shared apartment; your first rented home away from the family; a much cherished purchase after saving hard for a down payment; or one where you live alone, whether by choice or necessity, or with a partner, children, and increasingly other generations. It's our sanctuary from the world after the day's events, a place to restore our energies and find harmony. Therefore, the home should be a place of tranquility and, if we share it, unity.

Spells have been used for countless generations to keep our home safe from intruders, accidents, natural disasters, and quarrels within. Some of us have noisy, antisocial, or constantly complaining neighbors, who can make us feel as if we're under siege and make us dread coming home. Domestic spells are featured throughout the book in different chapters, as peace in the home is so central to our happiness and harmony.

In this chapter, we focus on spells to help you overcome many of the difficulties experienced in domestic life. Magical protection of the home will alleviate specific problems, but will also be ongoing, in the same way we lock our doors at night. And many of the old herbal charms adapt beautifully to the modern world, where we can buy them in the cooking aisle of the local supermarket.

To Leave Your Work Troubles
Outside the Home

YOU WILL NEED

A small bowl of dried flower petals or lavender- or rose-based potpourri ★ Dried sage in a small bowl ★ A small recyclable bag

TIMING

On returning home from work, ongoing

THE SPELL

* Place a bowl of dried flower petals and a bowl of sage by your front door.

* As you enter your home, drop dried petals from the bowl into the open bag, naming for each one a frustration or work worry.

* Sprinkle sage into the bag, saying, *Sage, take away bad experiences and worries of this day, that I may have peace, as the outer world I release.*

* Close and shake the bag six times, saying, *Absorb what must be left outside the door, that they will trouble me no more.*

* Open the front door and put the bag outside, so the contents can be thrown away in the morning, saying, *I welcome this peaceful time. Harmony at home shall be mine.*

To Avoid Taking Domestic Worries to Work

YOU WILL NEED

A bowl of cloves or juniper berries ★ A narrow piece of tinfoil ★ A bowl of salt ★ A bowl of pepper

TIMING

Before leaving home for work

THE SPELL

* Put nine cloves or juniper berries in the center of the tinfoil, touching each one, left to right, with the index finger of your dominant hand, and say for each, *Take in my angst, take in my fears. Absorb my domestic problems, sorrow, and tears.*

* Sprinkle salt over them, saying, *Cleansed be, let no distractions from home to work follow me.*

* Sprinkle pepper on top of the salt, saying, *Fade away, protected from all home worries, must I be this day.*

* Fold the tinfoil over the cloves into a parcel, making it as small as possible, and drop it in a garbage bin in or as near to the entrance of your workplace as you can.

To Protect Your Home from Intruders If You Are Frequently Away or Live in an Isolated Place

YOU WILL NEED

A raw egg ✳ A variety of seeds ✳ Sealing wax
or red sticky tape ✳ A small net bag

TIMING

During the end of the waning moon

THE SPELL

✳ Carefully cut the egg so that it has a small shell lid.

✳ Drain the egg and half-fill the larger part of the shell with seeds, saying,
Drive intruders from this place, with this magical shield, I you outface.
Inside here dwells a magick spell. Heed it well.

✳ Hold the part of the shell containing the seeds, shouting into it,
Begone, enter you shall not dare. Go instantly away I say, I care not where.

✳ Whisper in it the name of a fierce creature to stand guard.

✳ Replace the lid of the egg, sealing it with wax or tape, and put it in
the net bag.

✳ Hang the net bag over the front door or from a high window.

To Protect Your Home if There Has Been a Sudden Rash of Break-Ins or Vandalism in Your Area

A dragon's blood or spice incense stick ★ A shiny metal bowl in the center of your home, partly filled with a layer of potpourri, with three shiny new nails hidden in it (points facing down), followed by another layer of potpourri with three more nails hidden in it and a third similar layer

TIMING

Any of the three days leading to the full moon

THE SPELL

* Light the incense stick and, holding it like a smoke pen, draw in smoke doorways all around the bowl, saying, *Gates of iron, gates of steel, around my home your strength reveal. Gates of steel, gates of iron, impenetrable shall you be, to any who seek to enter maliciously.*

* When the fragrance fades, replace the potpourri, using the same nails.

Using Paper Dolls to Take Away All Negative Energies from Your Home and Family

YOU WILL NEED

A red pen ∗ Paper ∗ Scissors
∗ A heatproof pot or bucket

TIMING

The first day of spring

THE SPELL

∗ Draw a small outline of your home with the red pen on paper and cut it out. Then cut out paper dolls to represent each member of your family, including yourself and your pets.

∗ Within the paper house write all the domestic problems you're currently facing, including, for example, lack of money and noisy neighbors, and on each of the family member dolls any misfortunes, illness, quarrels, or losses occurring to them during the past twelve months.

∗ Hold each in turn, saying, *Within these paper symbols, I fix all sorrows, imprint loss and pain. We shall get rid of them with spring, and then begin again.*

∗ Drop the paper figures and the paper home in the heatproof pot outdoors, burn them, and scatter the ashes when cool in a garden.

Protection of Your Home Against Fire, Whether Accidental Fires, Explosions, Arson, Forest Fires, or Volcanoes

YOU WILL NEED

A red candle ★ A meteorite or a piece of lava

TIMING

A rainy day

THE SPELL

* Light the candle and pass the meteorite around it three times counterclockwise, three times clockwise, and three more times counterclockwise, saying, *Seheiah, angel who protects against destructive fire, accidental, deliberate, or nature inspired, guard my home from this day forth, from conflagration in south, east, west, and north.*

* Extinguish the candle and bury the meteorite near the property lines of where you live, in rain. If it is not raining, pour water on the ground where you have buried it.

Protection of Your Home Against Cyclones, Tornadoes, and Storms

YOU WILL NEED

Any blue tiger's eye or a more rare pietersite, called the "*tempest stone*," combining blue, gold, and brown tiger's eye ✳ A small wooden box with a lid and key

TIMING

When news of an imminent cyclone or other extreme stormy weather is forecast in your area

THE SPELL

✳ Take your crystal outdoors and stand in an exposed place, holding it high between your open cupped hands. Toss it three times, higher and higher each time, saying, *Zaamiel, angel of all tempestuous winds, let this storm/cyclone/tornado pass by. That my home may be sheltered by your billowing wings, preserve all from the whirling of the skies.*

✳ On the fourth throw, catch it and say, *Zaamiel, protect all, that we may not fall.*

✳ Lock the crystal in a dark place indoors until the threat has passed.

Protection of Your Home from Floods and Tidal Waves

YOU WILL NEED

A green or purple fluorite crystal or green jade or jasper,
called the "*rain stones*" ★ A bowl of water, preferably
rainwater ★ A gray candle ★ A bowl of soil

TIMING

When floods, high tides, or torrential rains are forecast

THE SPELL

* Dip the crystal into the water six times, saying the names of the angels of rain, *Ridya, Mathariel, let not the waters surge. My home and my area I entreat you preserve. Dry up the rains, send back the tides. Restore balance again. Let the defenses survive.*

* Pour the water onto the ground and embed the gray candle in the soil with the crystal pushed down in front of it. Light the candle and leave it to burn through.

* When the danger passes, wash the crystal and return the soil to where you found it.

Protection of Your Home from Earthquakes, Rock Slides, or Subsidence

209

YOU WILL NEED

A mustard-yellow candle ✳ A yellow jasper or mookaite crystal, set on top of a bowl of earth ✳ Mustard seeds

TIMING

When there are threats of danger

THE SPELL

✳ Light the candle and hold the bowl so the light catches it, saying, *Suiel, angel who protects against all quakes, hold steady this land, let it not shake. May it not shudder, collapse, and fall. Suiel, on your protection this day/night I call.*

✳ Press the crystal firmly into the earth in the bowl and scatter the mustard seeds on top, repeating the spell words.

✳ Bury it all in front of a big rock or put a rock on top of the mix, including the crystal, as you dig it into the earth, repeating the spell words a third time. Leave all in place, even when danger passes.

Protection Within Your Kitchen from Accidents, Such as Cuts, Falls, or Burns

Three blunt knives or scissors ＊ A shredded red candle ＊ A crumbled spice incense stick or cone ＊ A cloth bag ＊ Red cord or string

TIMING

Evening of the waning moon

THE SPELL

210

* Wrap the blunt implements, the shredded candle, and the incense in the cloth bag, tying it with nine knots and saying nine times, *All harm do I secure, Strong are the knots, long shall protection endure. Safe this kitchen from all accidents shall be, For seven long years, bound this shall be.*

* Put the sealed bag in a high cupboard for seven years, then throw it away and replace it.

To Prevent Falls on Stairs
if You Have Small Children
or Elderly Relatives

YOU WILL NEED

Red coral, turquoise, or amber—a small one for each
vulnerable family member ★ A very long pink scarf

TIMING

During the last days of the waning moon

THE SPELL

* Sit at the bottom of the stairs and hold each crystal in turn, naming
  the relative and saying, *Anauel, angel who protects against falls,
  for this loved one* [Name], *your protection I call.*

* Wrap the crystals tightly in the scarf and then knot it three times,
  saying, *Anauel, who protects those vulnerable against falls,
  may your protection be continually with them all.*

* Go to the top of the stairs with the knotted scarf and repeat,
  *Anauel, who protects those vulnerable against falls, may your protection
  be continually with them all.*

* Go downstairs again and keep the knotted scarf in a drawer as near
  as possible to the bottom of the stairs.

To Avoid Taking Any Sadness from Your Old Home or Picking Up Bad Energies from a New One

YOU WILL NEED

A dark stone found near your old home ⋆ Lavender seeds ⋆ A white stone found near your new home

TIMING

Before you leave your old home

THE SPELL

* Before leaving your old home, hold the dark stone inside, facing the open front door, and say, *Within this old home I leave all old sorrow, walking toward a bright tomorrow.*

* Stand outside, facing the open front door of the new home, holding the dark stone and say, *I draw out all sorrows from those who lived here before. I leave their troubles outside the door.*

* Bury the dark stone outside the new home and scatter lavender seeds on top.

* Place the white stone just inside the front door of your new home to bring in good energies from your old home to join any existing happiness waiting within.

To Protect Your Home from Family Quarrels and Sibling Rivalry

YOU WILL NEED

Small bowls of lavender or rose potpourri, one for each family member ✳ A larger, empty bowl in the area where the family meets ✳ Rose or lilac essential oil

TIMING

The start of a new week

THE SPELL

✳ Take a small quantity of potpourri from each family member's bowl in turn, adding it to the larger bowl.

✳ Mix the potpourri in the larger bowl, saying, *No more shall there be rivalry, backbiting, tantrums, or hostility. United shall we be as one family.*

✳ Add two or three drops of oil, saying, *Oil on troubled waters, peace henceforward shall there be. No more enmity.*

✳ Repeat the spell weekly.

✳ If any family member is disruptive, add extra oil to his/her bowl. Put his/her bowl outdoors in a sheltered place for 24 hours, saying, *Better mannered shall you be, if you want to be part of this family.*

To Clear a Home of Lingering Illness and Continual Minor Mishaps

YOU WILL NEED

A bowl of water with a large white flower head in it

TIMING

A sunny afternoon

THE SPELL

* Beginning with the room at the top back of the home and working your way to the front door, open each door and sprinkle water across the threshold. Then, in the flower water, draw the infinity symbol (see drawing) in the center of both sides of each door, ending with the outside of the front door.

* Say as you do so, *All that is not in healing or in harmony, removed shall be. Good health shall return, joyous fortune dwell. Once again within this home, all shall be well.*

* Pour the water outside the front door and keep the flower head in fresh water near the center of the home until it wilts.

If the Home Has Become a Hotel Where Family Members Just Pass Through

YOU WILL NEED

A central white candle, surrounded by small white candles for each person who lives in the home, including yourself

TIMING

An evening when you are alone

THE SPELL

* Light each of the small candles forming the circle clockwise in turn, and then hold each one briefly in the central candle, naming the family member, saying, *Draw back my family to the home's true heart, though life may take us far apart.*

* Blow softly into each candle in turn, saying, *A house is not a home, a home is what we share. I call you back in love and care, even if you're not often there.*

* Leave the candles to burn through. Try to arrange a time each week when everyone can gather, even briefly, and light their own candles.

If You Hate Your Present Home But Can't Move Away

YOU WILL NEED

Twelve walnuts ★ A gold bag

TIMING

Sunday morning

THE SPELL

* Holding one walnut, say, *Though this is not the right home for me, make me contented, while here I must be.*

* Whisper a wish for a move as soon as possible into the walnut, putting the walnut in the bag

* Then say, *The days grow shorter until I move, until then make this a place of love.*

* Each Sunday repeat the spell, adding a new wish walnut to the bag. When you have all twelve walnuts in the bag, hang the bag outside on a tree or bush, saying, *May the time I may move swiftly come. Until then make this a happy home.*

To Deter Noisy Neighbors
and Barking Dogs

YOU WILL NEED

Children's modeling clay ✳ Small red crystals
or stones ✳ Long red threads

TIMING

The end of a week or month

THE SPELL

✳ Make small figures with the modeling clay to represent your neighbors, dogs, yowling cats, etc., saying, *You* [name each one and their particular noise, e.g., roaring motorcycles, blaring television, etc.] *disturb my sanctuary, damage my sanity. And so you must, absolutely I trust, much quieter be.*

✳ Place a crystal in each mouth and/or tie the hands of serial hammerers, saying, *I've told you politely, asked you discreetly, with not even a frown. Now I take action, against your whole faction, I bind you completely, to keep the noise down.*

✳ Drive the figures to a distant crossroads, leave them there, and say, *Return when you learn.*

To Encourage Antisocial Neighbors to Move On

YOU WILL NEED

A bowl of fennel seeds, the seed of the traveler
★ A map of your county, your state, or the whole country

TIMING

Ongoing

THE SPELL

* Scatter fennel seeds over the map, saying, *Sorry you really have to go, you know, somewhere where others like you howl and clatter, yowl and scatter chaos through their lives. You really must move on, swiftly be gone, if I am to survive.*

* Carefully carry the map outdoors and pour the fennel seeds onto the ground, saying, *As far as possible away, your happy home where you shall stay. Where happy you can be, but best of all away from me.*

* Subtly scatter any remaining fennel seeds near or on your neighbors' property.

To Guard Your Home Against Loss, Sorrow, and Misfortune, and Encourage Abundance

YOU WILL NEED

A large garlic clove ✳ Brass tacks ✳ Copper pins ✳ Cloves ✳ Strong red thread to make a loop

TIMING

Evening by the light of a single small candle

THE SPELL

✳ Pierce the skin of the garlic clove with the brass tacks, saying, *Loss, sorrow, and misfortune, I give away here, removed from my home and those whom I hold dear. Bright in the morning light shall you shine, making abundance and good luck mine.*

✳ Add the copper pins to the garlic clove, repeating the spell words.

✳ Finally, add the cloves, saying the same spell words.

✳ Make a secure loop with the thread around the middle of the garlic clove, tying it firmly and tightly to a bush outdoors, where morning light will shine on it, until it decays.

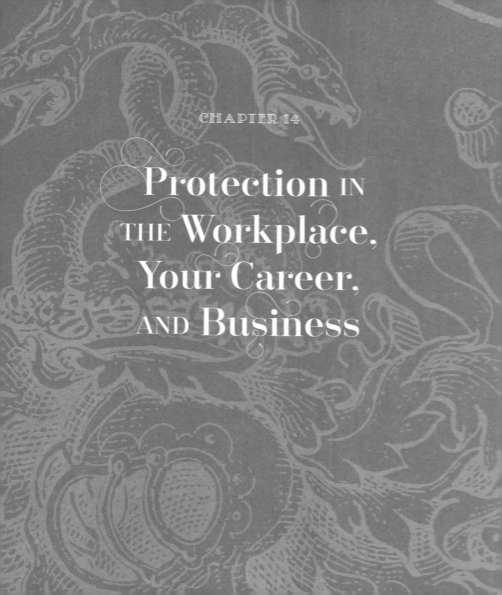

CHAPTER 14

Protection IN THE Workplace, Your Career, AND Business

Whether you run your own business or work for an organization, there are many ways you may need protection in an increasingly competitive workplace environment with pressure to deliver results fast. Working in a toxic atmosphere of backbiting and even bullying causes increasing absences through stress, and makes people dread going to work. And despite legislation banning them, sexism, ageism, and racism still exist.

Even in the caring professions, you often have to deal with a lack of staff and vast amounts of paperwork that make the job a bureaucratic nightmare. And unemployment brought on by redundancy can affect skilled workers, especially older ones, as the nature of work changes. These trends cause financial hardship as well as eroding self-confidence. Younger people, including new graduates, may find it hard to break into their chosen field.

Throughout this book you will find spells for workplace issues under different kinds of magick. This chapter offers a comprehensive selection to help with major issues, both in terms of protection and overcoming obstacles to employment and business success. Like the majority of spells in this book, it also replaces negativity with hope and positive results, for protection alone can leave gaps through which problems re-enter.

To Improve a Failing Business if You Feel Like Giving Up

· Dust from near an old anthill or termite hill ✶ Soil from as near to
your place of business as possible ✶ A small pot ✶ A twig,
also found as near to your business as possible ✶ Coriander
and cumin seeds, symbols of perseverance

TIMING

The first day of your workweek

THE SPELL

✶ Mix the dust and soil well, saying, *Ants/termites you work each day,
build, rebuild, never give way. I too will rebuild again and again,
my efforts shall not be in vain.*

✶ Place the dust and soil mixture in the pot, then write with the twig the
name of your business and the words BUSINESS I SAY, YOU SHALL REVIVE.
ONCE MORE SUCCESS SHALL COME ALIVE. It does not matter if you
cannot see the words.

✶ Keep the pot in your workplace and scatter the seeds daily for a
week outside.

If You Can't Get the Financial Rewards You Need and Deserve, in Business or Other Paid Employment

YOU WILL NEED

Any honey-flavored candies wrapped or unwrapped in another bag * A small bag of coins of any denomination

TIMING

During the waxing moon

THE SPELL

* Start out walking (or driving) where you know there are a series of crossroads. At the first one, drop three candies, saying, *May my future sweeter be, like honey. And extra financial rewards come rapidly.*

* At the second crossroads, drop three coins, repeating the spell words.

* Continue until you run out of candies/coins or crossroads.

If a Particular Job or Promotion
Seems Blocked to You,
No Matter What You Try

YOU WILL NEED

A silver key charm or a small silver-colored key on a chain

TIMING

Full moon

THE SPELL

* Hold the key by its chain outdoors on a full moon night, saying, *Mother Moon, give energy, to unlock the doors blocking me. Empower this key to open wide opportunity, and let me inside.*

* Hang the key on its chain from a tree or a bush, or an indoor plant by a window, until the morning, then wear it to work, saying the spell words every morning, noon, and evening as you touch it. Repeat the spell every full moon night until the doors open.

If a Company Takeover Is Imminent and You Fear for Your Job

YOU WILL NEED

A twig found on the shoreline ★ Seven white flowers and a gold hoop earring

TIMING

Just before high tide in the ocean or a tidal river

THE SPELL

❊ Just before high tide, draw a circle in the sand with a twig found on the shore, if possible, just below the high tide line, and set the flowers in the center of the circle. Inside the circle, around the edge, write the following so the words touch one another color: LADY OCEAN, MOTHER SEA, I ASK YOU NOT TO HOLD BACK INEVITABILITY. BUT TO KEEP MY JOB SAFE FOR ME.

❊ Cast the gold hoop earring into the water, saying, *This offering of gold to you I bring. As the tides flow, let the danger of this takeover to me go. That I may remain secure, and my present employment long endure.*

❊ Leave the shore and don't look back.

An Alternative Fire Version to Keep Your Job if There Is a Takeover

YOU WILL NEED

A piece of smooth wood ⋆ A sharp knife or etching tool
⋆ A heatproof pot half-filled with sand outdoors or a bonfire

TIMING

As close to the full moon during the waxing period as possible

THE SPELL

* On the wood, etch the first letter of each of these words: KEEP MY JOB SAFE IN UNCERTAIN TIMES.

* Burn the wood in the heatproof pot or a bonfire, saying, *Power of fire, rise ever higher. Make my work secure, and my future prospects there endure. That I shall be part, of a different and better start.*

If Your Job Has Been Made Redundant and You Cannot Find Another Job

A basil plant, the herb of prosperity and good employment, in a pot ∗ Dried basil in a bowl ∗ A blue permanent waterproof marker

TIMING

When you are applying for other jobs

THE SPELL

∗ Surround the basil plant with ever-widening circles of dried basil. Draw in pen on the pot surface the raku lightning flash symbol (see drawing) that represents bringing what is most needed into the everyday world from the heavens.

∗ Say, *Open to me, pastures new. Experience, expertise, I offer to you. Whoever will give me opportunity, I will prove what an asset I can be.*

∗ Cast the rest of the dried basil outdoors, saying, *I send out my needs, far and wide. My wisdom and knowledge, I shall not hide.*

∗ Tend the plant. When you land an interview, carry three basil leaves in a small bag.

To Right Injustice in the Workplace if You Are Experiencing Hidden or Overt Ageism, Sexism, or Racism

229

YOU WILL NEED

Lemon juice ⁕ A small jug of water

TIMING

Beginning Wednesday evening for five days

THE SPELL

⁕ Pour five drops of lemon juice into the water, saying, *This prejudice leaves a sour taste, my talents daily go to waste. I call* [name the prejudice and the worst perpetrators] *to account, to put right these injustices too numerous to count.*

⁕ Pour away the lemon water, saying, *Value me for my ability, for what I do, not who you see. I dilute your prejudice, toward me.*

⁕ Each night add one fewer drop of juice to a fresh jug of water, repeating the spell exactly.

⁕ On day 6, pour plain water on plants, saying, *Injustices are gone, the future clear. I claim my rights, for all to hear.*

⁕ Take a bottle with five drops of lemon juice to work, sipping a little before tackling issues.

For Protection from Someone Who Takes a Totally Irrational Dislike to You in a New or Existing Workplace

YOU WILL NEED

A heatproof, sealable thermos, filled with boiling water ✳ Sugar

TIMING

A day you are not at work

THE SPELL

* Mix into the thermos two teaspoons of sugar, saying, [Name], *sweeter be, treat me not so venomously.*

* Keep adding teaspoons of sugar until no more will dissolve, saying, *Remove your dislike, your irrational spite. With sugar niceness, I pour into you. When we next meet, let kindness flood through.*

* Put the lid on the thermos and empty as much of the contents as possible near an ant or termite nest or where flies are buzzing.

* Wash out the thermos.

* When you are at work, offer to make a drink for the person who has shown dislike toward you, saying the words as you mix it. If s/he refuses, say the spell words when you next see her/him drinking.

To Reduce Constant Pressure to Reach Impossible Deadlines

YOU WILL NEED
A small clock with a loud tick

TIMING
When your workplace is deserted

THE SPELL

* Stop the clock near your inbox, computer, or wherever you are overloaded most, saying, *Stop the clock racing relentlessly. I will no longer be driven by it mercilessly.*

* Put the clock away in a drawer, leave the workplace right away, do something relaxing, and return an hour later.

* Restart the clock, saying, *You do not rule nor own me. I set the pace. No more shall others pressure me or make me race.*

* State your realistic deadlines. Keep the clock in a work drawer so, when you feel pressure increasing, you can stop it for an hour.

A Second Clock Spell to Avoid Making Mistakes Under Pressure

A watch

Whenever you realize that you have made a mistake due to pressure

* Sit in your workplace/stationary vehicle and set the watch back an hour, saying, *Time, move back gradually, until all is put right. Though time is tight, stand still. So no one will, notice this error but me.*

* Fix the mistake as best and rapidly as you can, then put the watch time forward, saying, *Mistakes undone, errors gone. Accuracy is regained, and no one blamed.*

* Do this while repeating the spell words whenever you feel you are being rushed into making errors.

To Protect Yourself in a Toxic Workplace, Where There are Constant Absences, Stress-Related Illnesses, and High Personnel Turnover

YOU WILL NEED

Three small, round amethysts ✳ Two small bowls of water ✳ Three small, pointed, clear quartz crystals ✳ A healthy green plant, preferably mint, as a barrier in your workspace

TIMING

Daily

THE SPELL

✳ Soak the amethysts in one bowl and the quartz crystals in the other, and set them in front of the plant in your workspace.

✳ Each morning sprinkle the plant and your own brow, throat, and inner wrist points with, first, the amethyst water and, then, the quartz water, saying, *Be for me sanctuary, against stress, sickness, and drains on my energy. Heal the workplace, strengthen me, That by this toxic environment unaffected shall I be.*

✳ Pour away the remaining water on any workplace plants at the end of the day and refill the bowls, adding the crystals before leaving work.

To Protect Yourself if You Work in a Soulless Environment

YOU WILL NEED

A circle of seven small candles, set in the following order: red, orange, yellow, green, blue, purple, and white ★ Seven crystals, one in each color, set in a circle around the candles

TIMING

During the waxing moon

THE SPELL

* In your home, light each candle in the order specified above, saying, *Call to me this shining rainbow, that within and from me you shall glow. Bring enthusiasm to my task, This I ask.*

* Blow out the candles fast in reverse order, saying, *Awaken my soul sleeping within, let the rainbow light flood in.*

* Take the crystals to work and arrange them in a semicircle in your workspace, red first and white last. Touch each in turn every morning, saying, *I awaken my soul sleeping within, I let the shining rainbow in.*

To Protect Yourself from Undue Aggression and Cliques When Working in Markets and Fairs

YOU WILL NEED

Two dark, pointed crystals and two clear,
pointed ones * A sagebrush smudge stick or,
if not allowed, a blue or gray feather

TIMING

Before you set up your booth

THE SPELL

* Claim your space and set up your booth, politely greeting everyone around you.

* Place your four crystals in a close square, alternately dark and light, in the center of your booth.

* Light your smudge stick or hold the feather, subtly wafting them around your booth to make a smoke or visualized square, including where customers will sit or stand. Say softly and continuously, *You are welcome here, all who bring and spread good cheer. But barred are you whose market you hate to share, and would prefer I was not there.*

* Extinguish the smudge stick and put your crystals at the corners of the booth, alternating colors, facing outward, the dark to repel hostility and the light to encourage business.

To Protect Yourself from Psychic Attack When Working in a Supposedly Spiritual Environment

YOU WILL NEED

Eucalyptus or tea tree oil
★ Absorbent cotton squares ★ A saucer

TIMING

When you are working in the same space or building with other psychics, therapists, or healers who resent you

THE SPELL

* Place a drop of oil on the index and middle fingers of your dominant hand.

* With those two fingers together and your hand and arm outstretched, palm flat and facing down, turn in every direction from the center of your own space/room, saying, *Spiritual Mafia, come not near, you know just who you are. Your nasty spells I do not fear, your ill wishes I do bar. I am here to stay. And if you don't like it, you can go away.*

* Put a few drops of oil on absorbent cotton squares on a saucer in a warm place in your room/space.

To Protect Your Business and Yourself from Being Squeezed by Increasingly Unreasonable Demands from Ruthless Landlords or Their Representatives

YOU WILL NEED

A lidded glass jar ✳ Fresh rosemary, mixed, if possible, with rue ✳ Sharp objects ✳ Apple cider vinegar ✳ Strong red tape

TIMING

At the beginning of the new moon cycle

THE SPELL

✳ Line the bottom and sides of the jar with rosemary/rue and in the center put a layer of sharp objects followed by an insulating layer of rosemary/rue. If the landlord's demands are getting really nasty, add a few broken glass shards (carefully).

✳ Almost fill the jar with apple cider vinegar and seal it with red tape, shaking it nine times with the lid secured.

✳ Say, *You who make my life so hard, with relentless demands and threatened barbs, that send me backwards financially. No more shall you threaten me.*

✳ Place the jar in a dark spot, saying, *In this jar your ruthlessness I seal, my peace of mind no more like my profits can you steal.*

To Persuade Potential Investors/Banks to Take a Chance on You if They Are Expressing Doubts

YOU WILL NEED

A crystal or glass dish, piled with small, gold-colored items with your business card on top ★ Frankincense essential oil, diluted in olive oil ★ Six gold candles in a row behind the dish

TIMING

Sunday, toward the full moon

THE SPELL

* Run the index finger of your dominant hand around the inside rim of the dish, using a drop or two of oil.

* Light the candles, left to right, saying, *See only this shield of gold, prosperity in my venture shall you behold.*

* Blow out the candles, right to left, saying, *Your refusal and doubts I do not need, I shall succeed with your support indeed. Protected by this golden light, I seize the chance to prove I'm right.*

* Leave the business card with the gold items and take it to any meeting with investors or bankers.

When Your Business Survival is at Stake

Red chalk * A children's chalkboard
* An eraser * White chalk

TIMING

When things are looking dire

THE SPELL

* Write in red chalk all over the chalkboard, THERE IS NO OPTION LEFT, YET I CANNOT, WILL NOT FAIL. I CALL ON ALL SOURCES ABOVE AND HERE, PROTECT ME FROM FEAR, FOR I MUST AND CAN PREVAIL.

* Erase the words and hold the board to any light, saying, *Survive and thrive, the business still can come alive.*

* In white chalk, write in the center of the board, WINNER TAKES ALL, I WILL NOT FALL.

* Go out there and fight.

For a Well-Deserved Promotion Interview, When You Know Bias May Color the Choice

A ladle * A kitchen scale with a pan on
either side * A jar of uncooked rice

TIMING

The week before the interview

THE SPELL

* Using a ladle, almost fill one pan of the scale with rice so the scale dips, saying, *The odds are stacked against me, yet shall I gain fair chance. Favoritism, hidden influence, I dismiss them with a glance.*

* Scoop sufficient rice into the other pan so that the two pans balance, saying, *An even chance, a level playing field. When my expertise shall be revealed, all bias will toward me yield.*

* Continue heaping rice in the pan, saying, *Yet with friends in high places, inequality may sneak right back. Equal-handed Justice, may you protect me, giving me the support I lack.*

* Cook a meal using some of the empowered rice and then again the night before the interview.

If You Need to Retrain Within Your Career or a New Job and Fear Failing

YOU WILL NEED

Two mint tea bags in a pot of hot water ★ A spoon
★ A mug ★ A large bowl ★ A printout page or photocopy
of material you must learn ★ A mint plant

TIMING

When you are relaxed

THE SPELL

* Stir the tea seven times clockwise, pour some in the mug, and sip it, saying, *I release my abilities, to learn and master all I see. In future days, and brand new ways, Easy-peasy, Jack-a reasy.*

* Pour the rest of the tea into the bowl and immerse the printout in the bowl, saying, *Absorb new material, easily and thoroughly I will, saturate myself with learning. And better bucks soon be earning, Easy-peasy, Jack-a reasy.*

* Before the paper disintegrates, pour a little of the bowl's contents into a hole dug beneath a thriving mint plant and dispose of the rest.

* Finish your tea and start studying, saying, *Easy-peasy, Jack-a reasy.*

CHAPTER 15

Protection
While Traveling
AND Commuting

With ever-faster trains and planes; long-distance buses rolling across the United States, Australia, and Europe; and cruise ships opening up the world, travel is no longer the sole province of the rich. There are many budget vacation packages available. However, these bring accompanying hazards, rare but worrying crashes, and fears, especially with the threat of terrorism ever-present. Likewise, commuting holds its hazards: as extra traffic causes delays, this sometimes prompts unreasonable anger from frustrated motorists taking out their frustrations on other motorists. For those who drive regularly, whether to or for work, others' carelessness or their own tiredness or a momentary lapse in concentration can lead to accidents and even fatalities.

Spells to protect travelers have been a mainstay through countless generations. In addition to using the medallion of St. Christopher, the patron saint of travelers, this chapter also calls for the use of crystals related to different aspects of travel. Once empowered as talismans, these are excellent to carry, but you can substitute a clear quartz crystal for active protection, an amethyst for gentler energies, or a pearl or any shining glass nugget or bead of the same color. Cast protective travel spells on behalf of loved ones as well as yourself by slightly adapting the words or adding their names if you are traveling together.

Protection by Archangel Raphael if You Commute or Drive Regularly or for a Living

YOU WILL NEED

A purple kunzite or green and white dendritic (tree) agate ★ Comfrey leaves (or split a comfrey tea bag), fennel seeds, and ground ginger ★ A dark blue bag

TIMING

The day before your workweek begins

THE SPELL

* Place the crystal and half the comfrey, fennel seeds, and ginger in the bag, close it, shake it five times, and say, *The roads are perilous, each day more dangerous. Raphael Archangel, guardian of the highways, slow and winding or fast freeway, be for me my daily guide. Through all hazards stay by my side.*

* Put the bag under the driver's seat. As you begin your first journey every week, scatter a little of the herb mix out the driver's side window, saying, *There and back, day by day, protect me on my journey's way.*

* Make more mix as needed, empowering the mix with the second set of spell words.

Protection from Aggressive Driving or Aggressive Behavior by Other Motorists

YOU WILL NEED

Four fire or blood agates, red tiger's eye,
or any small red crystals ★ A small net

TIMING

Before a major journey

THE SPELL

* Hold two crystals in each closed hand and raise your arms over your head, then down behind your back, then bring your arms around to your front and upward in a slashing movement and then slowly down to your sides, saying, *Let none show anger, none express rage, become uncontrolled or at me be outraged. Calm must disarm.*

* Drop the crystals in the net, saying, *So I catch all rage and outrage, aimed against my vehicle and me. Disarmed, defused, silenced be.*

* Keep the net of crystals in the glove compartment of the vehicle and, before any major journey or highway driving, where you may encounter aggressive drivers, hold the net and repeat the second set of spell words.

If Your Teenager Has Just Started Driving Unaccompanied and is Reckless

YOU WILL NEED

Holy/sacred water bought online from a religious site, from a sacred well, or made with nine pinches of salt stirred into a bowl of water with a silver letter opener and a cross made on the surface ∗ A St. Christopher medallion or car magnet

TIMING

Saturday evening

THE SPELL

∗ Sprinkle sacred water over the medallion, saying, *Wise St. Christopher, into your hands I place my beloved child, who is unwise. Be for him/her ears and eyes. Slow speed, make him/her heed.*

∗ Sprinkle sacred water drops around the medallion, saying, *Hold my child safely, protected from danger, from overconfidence and careless stranger.*

∗ Give your child the medallion to wear or hang in the car.

∗ Sprinkle sacred water around the car keys.

∗ Keep the rest of the sacred water by a picture of your teenager with the car.

To Protect Against Inattention Due to Tiredness or a Momentary Lapse While Driving

YOU WILL NEED

A lemon, pine, or fern fragrant air freshener to hang in the vehicle * Ground ginger, allspice, saffron, and turmeric * Talcum powder or cornstarch * The same essential oil as the air freshener

TIMING

The beginning of a new week

THE SPELL

* Mix together the ginger, allspice, saffron, and turmeric, plus the talcum powder or cornstarch and a drop or two of the essential oil, using sufficient talcum powder or cornstarch to make the herbs blend together, and say, *Keep me awake, attentive, alert, that I and other road users may not be hurt, by my losing concentration, and causing an accident through hesitation.*

* Scatter the mix around the air freshener on a flat surface, repeating the spell words, and pour the rest of the mix near the point where the vehicle begins the journey.

* Hang the air freshener in the vehicle. If the vehicle is a motorcycle or a bicycle, hang the air freshener where you store the vehicle.

Protection from Accidents and Attacks While Traveling on Trains, Buses, Boats, and Planes

A small electric fan * Tickets, or printouts of boarding passes from future or past journeys * A bowl of earth * The ash of a burned lavender incense cone * A small bowl of water

TIMING

Wednesday

THE SPELL

* Pass the fan, set on medium speed, gently over the tickets so they do not blow away, saying, *May this journey be smooth and without incident. By sky, land, or water, may protection be sent.*

* Slow the fan speed so the papers hardly move, saying, *Peaceful, tranquil, and calm, free from disasters, accidents, and harm.*

* Mix together the earth, ash, and a little water, saying, *By Earth and Sea and Sky be blessed. By day and night, may all stay right.*

* Scatter the mix on the ground as you leave home or right after a family member departs.

Protection from Bicycle and Motorcycle Crashes and Falls

YOU WILL NEED

A length of tinfoil ★ A turquoise or
green amazonite ★ A pink scarf

TIMING

Weekly, on a Monday

THE SPELL

* Take the foil and crush it hard, saying, *Foil take the impact of any fall, any damage now absorb, so future accidents cannot happen at all.*

* Wrap the crushed foil around the turquoise, place it in the pink scarf, and knot the scarf firmly, saying, *Wrapped in protection shall you/I be, permanently. Free from danger on the highway, safe from crashes, falls, collisions, secure by night and day.*

* Keep the knotted scarf high in the place where the bicycle/motorcycle is stored.

Protection from Travel-Related Terrorism in Crowded Places You May Visit

YOU WILL NEED

A photo(s) of yourself/those traveling
* Twenty-eight small black stones

TIMING

Three days before the onset of travel

THE SPELL

* Around the photo(s), set a square of four stones, then around that eight in a square, and a third square of sixteen around the outside, saying, *This triple wall protects all, three by three, against terrorism on Land, Sky, or Sea. Let slaughtering of innocents cease. May there be peace.*

* Remove the outermost square of stones, one by one, casting them into water and saying, *Let places of leisure be filled with pleasure, may travel be free from hostility. That fear may become a thing of the past, and harmless bystanders no more be lost.*

* On day 2, remove the middle layer, repeating the second set of spell words.

* Leave the innermost square in place while you travel.

A Second Antiterrorism Protection Spell if You or a Loved One are Going to a Particularly Dangerous Part of the World

YOU WILL NEED

Five lemongrass or spice incense cones,
in a row, on a plate

TIMING

Whenever extra warnings are issued

THE SPELL

* Light the first cone and, when it is burned, crush the ash on the plate, saying, *Safe from terrorism shall you/I be, though you/I travel perilously, on Land, in the Sky, or at Sea.*

* Continue lighting the incense cones, left to right, repeating the actions and the spell words.

* When all are ash, scatter a third of the ash to the winds, cast a third in water, and bury the rest.

To Protect Luggage, Electronic Devices, and Travel Documents, Using a Viking Rune during Travel and While on Vacation

THE SPELL

✳ On each label and on the crystal, trace invisibly using the index finger of your dominant hand, the Viking rune Thurisaz, the protective hammer of the thunder god Thor (see drawing). Say, *May the mighty Hammer of Thor drive away all thieves. That they will leave, untouched all that is precious to me. May there be no loss, no damage, no partings of possessions from me, accidentally or maliciously.*

✳ Label everything as usual, but as you attach the labels repeat the spell words. Draw the rune invisibly on labels before your return journey.

If You or a Family Member are Relocating Far Away and Fear Losing Touch

Two identical necklaces with crystals
between the chain links

TIMING

Before you/the person leave(s)

THE SPELL

* Fasten the necklaces together and touch each crystal in turn, saying,
  [Name], *we are one. In love are we joined as family, united heart to heart
  though far in distance may we be. No ocean wide, nor endless Sky,
  nor vast tract of land, shall break this bond and band.*

* Separate the necklaces and give one necklace to the other person
  to hang by his computer/communication device and hang yours in
  the room where you will be communicating with him through
  cyberspace/the phone.

* Each time, before connecting, touch each bead and repeat the
  spell words.

If You Want to Travel or Relocate Overseas, But Obstacles Constantly Appear

YOU WILL NEED

Four mint or lavender incense sticks ✳ A map, including where you live and where you want to go ✳ A row of eight dark stones, leading from your present location on the map to the desired destination ✳ Eight citrine or any small yellow crystals

TIMING

During the full moon

THE SPELL

* Leave the map and citrines where sunlight enters.

* Place the incense sticks in a square. The incense stick furthest away from you on the left is number 1. The incense stick furthest away from you on the right is number 3. The incense stick nearest you on the left is number 2, and the incense stick nearest you on the right is number 4.

* Light the incense sticks, left to right, top to bottom.

* Spiral incenses 1 and 3, 2 and 4, 1 and 4, 2 and 3 around the edges of the map, saying, *Wide the distance, far to go, yet I decree, it can be so. I take away an obstacle.*

* Take away a black stone and replace it with a citrine.

* Continue to take away dark stones, saying, *I take away an obstacle,* replacing with them with citrines.

* Discard the black stones.

If You are Saying Goodbye to a Backpacking Family Member and are Very Anxious About Her/His Safety

A small cloth tag to attach inside the backpack or on an outer garment being worn ★ A permanent marker ★ A green candle ★ Needle and thread or fabric fixative

THE SPELL

* On the tag, draw the protective symbol Harth, the gateway (see drawing).

* By the light of the candle, affix the tag, saying, *Protected by me devotedly, may Adnachiel, voyager angel, also with you be. May the road be kind, and good shelter find, no harm befall. Secure protection all the way until once more I see, you home in victory.*

* Blow out the candle and every night light a green candle before s/he will be going to bed, renewing your protection.

To Protect Your Possessions from Theft and Yourself from Mugging, Spiked Drinks, or Harassment While on Vacation

257

YOU WILL NEED

A St. Christopher medallion on a chain

TIMING

Before going out for the first time

THE SPELL

* Hold the medallion between your closed hands, saying,
  Good St. Christopher, who through centuries past, on all travelers your guardianship have cast, you who shield travelers in need, I ask that this my request you heed. That on my vacation on every occasion, you offer me protection from each direction.

* Turn around clockwise to face the four directions, saying,
  St. Christopher protect me against all harm, from east, south, north, and west, guard me in the way you know is best.

* Open your hands and breathe on the medallion to endow it with your essence and wear it until you return home.

To Protect Yourself from Becoming Ill During a Journey or While on Vacation

YOU WILL NEED

A mug ✳ A chamomile or mint tea bag ✳ A green jade crystal

TIMING

The day before the journey

THE SPELL

✳ Make a mug of chamomile or mint tea, stirring three times clockwise and three times counterclockwise, and say, *Keep me well, keep me strong, keep away illness, day and night long, that my vacation will be pure pleasure, days of wellness I can treasure.*

✳ Sip the tea, repeating the spell words.

✳ As the tea becomes cooler, dip the jade into the tea, saying the same spell words.

✳ Wash the jade in clear water and drink the rest of the tea, saying, *Health and strength shall me surround, no hint of illness be around. Well shall I be and well remain, all the way there* [name destination] *and home again.*

✳ Take the jade with you.

To Avoid Being Conned on Vacation Financially, by False Lovers or Parasitic New "Friends"

YOU WILL NEED

Your travel documents, credit cards, and overseas currency ✳ A blue or red tiger's eye ✳ Three yellow candles, set in a triangle ✳ Dried lemongrass in a bag

TIMING

Any Wednesday before the vacation

THE SPELL

* Place your travel documents, credit cards, and overseas currency, plus the tiger's eye, in the center of the candle triangle, together with the lemongrass bag.

* Light the candles clockwise, starting with the one nearest to you, and say, *Shield me financially, protect me emotionally, from all who would cheat, con, and mislead. Thwart those who smile, as they commit their misdeeds.*

* Blow out the candles.

* Shake the closed lemongrass bag outdoors five times, saying, *Against human snakes, keep all safe.*

* Scatter the lemongrass, saying, *Begone all cons, come not near. Sneaky ones, begone.*

* Keep the tiger's eye in your purse or wallet while you're on vacation.

To Avoid Travel Delays and Disruption

A dark blue cord or ribbon ★ Printouts of your
travel documents and hotel bookings

TIMING

When you are packed for travel

THE SPELL

* Tie five loose knots in the cord and wrap it loosely with an extra single knot around printouts of your travel documents and hotel bookings.

* Untie the documents and undo the first knot in the cord, saying, *Smooth be, disruption free.*

* Untie the second cord knot, saying, *Through any security, swift and unchallenged shall I/we be.*

* Undo the third cord knot, saying, *Travel delays, flow and fly away.*

* Undo the fourth cord knot, saying, *Good conditions across Land/Sea/Sky, smooth and calm, no cause for alarm.*

* Undo the fifth cord knot, saying, *Arrived safe and sound, looking all around. Perfect weather, it's all come together.*

* Carry the unknotted cord with you on the journey.

To Protect an Older Child or Teenager Going Away on a School Journey or with Friends

YOU WILL NEED

Powdered washing detergent, containing lavender or chamomile fragrance (unless the child is allergic to one of those scents) ✴ Your child's favorite garment ✴ A green jade or turquoise crystal ✴ A photo of your child

TIMING

A week before the trip

THE SPELL

* Wash and dry the garment, and wrap the crystal inside it for the week before the trip.

* Daily hold the garment with the crystal inside, saying, *Keep safe from getting lost or hurt, from danger and accident of every sort. From risk taking and mistake-making, I enfold you. Elemiah, angel of safe travel, stand strong and true.*

* Pack the garment.

* Keep the crystal with your child's photo while s/he is away and repeat the spell words nightly.

For Night Workers and All Who Travel Alone Late at Night

Silver candles ✳ A silver purse or bag ✳ A creamy moonstone,
pearl or white selenite ✳ Your door key and car keys if you drive

TIMING

On a full moon night

THE SPELL

* Stand in full moonlight or, if it's cloudy, light three silver candles indoors.

* Hold the purse to the light, saying, *Shine bright moonlight, that night may become as clear as day, in lonely places, against angry faces, predators and mobs. Protect all of us whose lives and jobs, expose us to the perils of the night. Lady Moon, hold us tight.*

* Leave the purse in a sheltered place in moonlight all night or indoors until the candles burn down.

* Carry the crystal with your keys at night.

* Every Monday before work, light a silver candle briefly next to your keys and crystal within the purse, repeating the spell words.

To Protect You if You Stay in Unfamiliar Places or Hotels on Business

YOU WILL NEED

A photo of yourself at home
(with any loved ones if you wish)

TIMING

When you reach your hotel room

THE SPELL

* Set the photo by the bed and, as it gets dark, switch on any lamps (not the main light).

* Putting your hands around the photo, say, *Make this a home away from home, that I will rest peacefully, safely, quietly, a sanctuary, until once more I home shall be.*

* Hold the photo to your heart.

* Repeat the spell words and actions after making any contact with home and before you go to sleep, switching off the lamps one by one.

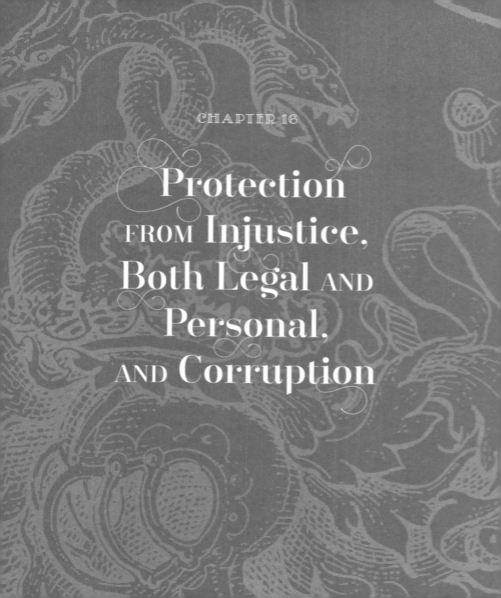

CHAPTER 16

Protection
FROM Injustice,
Both Legal AND
Personal,
AND Corruption

I njustice comes in many forms—unfairness at work, scapegoating by our family, constantly being passed over at work for promotion, family custody or inheritance disputes, or a parent with a serious drug problem or a tendency to violence may be given custody, and we know the situation is potentially dangerous or distressing to the child. The following justice spells address both personal and legal or official matters that may overlap. A lawyer may be incompetent or merely interested in taking increasing amounts of money from us with no results, there may be seemingly impossible delays in court hearings, and no one may be listening. Sometimes the law may seem totally biased, allowing the guilty to walk away and leaving the innocent to pick up the pieces.

Justice spells are useful when we have tried everything—practically and legally—and have hit an impasse. They can offer protection for us and loved ones from corruption, unfairness, and indifference, and remove obstacles and unfair attacks on us, thereby galvanizing legal authorities to take appropriate action. Indeed, just by changing the name and a few spell words, you can use every spell to defend those you love. Once you have cast the spell a few times, you will gain renewed strength and authority to triumph in your cause.

To Overcome Injustice from the Past That is Eating Away at You

An apple or pear that is going brown and soft
* A bowl

TIMING

During the last day of the waning moon

THE SPELL

* Cut the fruit into pieces, dropping each discarded piece into the bowl and saying, *Decaying injustices, that cannot be put right, that eat me away by day and by night. Yet no matter how painfully and often I recall, cannot change the past at all.*

* As the remaining fruit becomes progressively smaller, keep repeating the spell words softly.

* When pared down to the core and seeds, bury these, saying, *The future shall grow, letting go of what cannot be mended. Yesterday's injustices are ended.*

* Buy and eat a new piece of fruit.

To Protect Yourself from Ongoing Injustices While You Try to Change Them

YOU WILL NEED

As many beads as there are injustices ✳ A water-soluble red pen or paint ✳ A fine paintbrush ✳ A string sufficiently long to hang over a tap and to be splashed by the water when it is turned on

TIMING

Evening during the waning moon

THE SPELL

✳ Take each bead and name an injustice. On it paint the Viking rune for justice, Tiwaz (see drawing), saying for each, *Though daily these injustices I must now endure, before long shall they be removed, that's for sure. Step by step and day by day, I wash injustice clean away.*

✳ Leave the beads to dry and thread them on the string, hanging them over a tap until the symbols dissolve. Wash them well and, even if they're stained, hang them in the location where the injustices occur. As each is resolved, remove a bead.

If You are Taken for Granted at Work and Always Passed Over for Promotion or a Raise

YOU WILL NEED

An old broom at home ✱ Dried star anise or cloves
in a bowl, mixed with gold or silver stars

TIMING

Three or four days before the full moon

THE SPELL

✱ Hold the broom and say, *As useful am I as this old broom, taken for granted, not seen in a room. Others less able gain promotion and money, useful old broom, it's no longer funny.*

✱ Sweep the star anise and stars out the front door with the broom, saying, *New brooms sweep clean, this is the last of this old broom that ever shall be seen. Promote me now, more money vow, or I'll be on my way, to find appreciation and not stay.*

✱ Buy a new broom and consign the old one to the garden/yard.

✱ Collect the star anise and stars from outside the house and dispose of them in a refuse bin.

If You are Always the Scapegoat in Your Family, No Matter What You Say or Do

A children's toy goat or fashion one out of modeling clay

Before a family get-together

* Hold the goat and say, *Your scapegoat I have been for too many years, blamed for your anger and shed many tears. But like the scapegoat who was in the desert set free, I now declare I'll liberate me.*

* Leave the goat in a barren place or wasteland and buy yourself a silver Capricorn goat charm or medallion to remind you of your transformation.

To Get Justice When Your Child or Children Have Been Taken Away to Another Country and You are Being Denied Custody

YOU WILL NEED

A small branch with growing leaves ∗ Biodegradable luggage tags or strips of paper with a string attached

TIMING

Wednesday, the day of Raphael, archangel of the four winds

THE SPELL

∗ Plant the branch in an open place, saying, *Winds of the Earth, blow over the Sea. Restore my lost children, once more to me.*

∗ Write on each label a child's name, saying, *Winds of the Sea, bring my lost children back home to me.*

∗ Attach each label to the branch, saying for each one, *Winds of the Air, bring back my lost children, to my loving care.*

∗ Walk away, saying, *I send my love across the Sea. Beloved children let justice be, that you shall soon be restored to me.*

For Challenging a Child Custody Decision When You Know the Other Parent is a Danger to the Children, But No One Believes You

YOU WILL NEED

A photo of your ex ∗ A black permanent marker ∗ Scissors ∗ Echinacea powder

TIMING

A week before the court hearing

THE SPELL

∗ On the photo, draw a black mask over your ex's eyes, saying, *You hide your evil intentions well, a loving personality to the courts you sell.*

∗ Cut out the mask from the picture, saying, *I take away your mask. All I ask is that you are seen in your true face. Not Mr./Ms. Nice Guy, but a dangerous disgrace.*

∗ Dispose of the remaining face in the bottom of a cat litter tray or flushed in small pieces down the toilet, saying, *Stay away, from today.*

∗ Hang the mask where sunlight will shine on it.

For Getting Your Rights in an Acrimonious Divorce, When You Don't Have the Strength to Fight On

YOU WILL NEED

White paper * Rainbow-colored erasable pencils * An eraser * Scissors * A padded envelope

TIMING

Before a hearing

THE SPELL

* Draw on half the paper a white outline of yourself and on the other half your ex's outline in black, saying, *I feel that I am disappearing, losing my power, you* [Name], *wear me down, day by day, in every way, and hour by hour.*

* Erase the outline of yourself and redraw your whole outline in blue and fill it with rainbow colors, saying, *Stop, no more, I know the score. You know my buttons to press, under duress. But my new power does grow, soon you will know.*

* Cut away the dark figure, saying, *Gone from the equation, your bullying persuasion.*

* Put the dark figure in a padded envelope, dumping it in a garbage bin outside the court.

To Overcome Injustice by Ruthless People Who are Threatening to Evict You from Your Home or Close Down Your Business

A red candle in a deep holder ★ An incense stick
in sandalwood or sage ★ A bowl of salt

TIMING

Thursday

THE SPELL

* Light the candle and the incense from the candle, saying, *Fire grow, fire glow. Power and justice shall be so. By the power of the Fire, so it shall be as I desire against* [name threat and people]. *The fires of justice grow ever higher.*

* Cast a pinch of salt into the candle flame, saying, *Salt sparkle, fire crackle and inspire, by the power of justice and of Fire* [name desired outcome].

* Using the incense stick like a smoke pen, write in the air the desired outcome around the outside of the candle, saying, *The power is free, justice shall I see, justice shall come as I desire, by the blazing power of Fire.*

* Let the candle burn through and wash the remaining salt away under a running tap, saying, *Water added to Fire flows free, bringing justice I shall see.*

A Spell to Overcome Corrupt People Who Use Their Official Position or Wealth to Trample Your Rights

Fast-growing grass seed ✷ An eggshell
✷ Cotton squares ✷ Small scissors

TIMING

When your grass has grown

THE SPELL

* Scatter the grass seed, water it, and watch as it grows.

* Once the grass has started growing, line the eggshell with cotton squares that you're constantly moistening.

* Crush the eggshell and say, *You who use corrupt power and position, I reverse your decision, and your derision. I will cut you down to size.*

* Mow the grass, saying, *Cut down to size, no longer shall corruption rise. Small my spell, But cast so well, I get rid of you with this eggshell.*

* Place the crushed eggshell into the ground and any remaining grass.

* Repeat weekly until you feel you have achieved your objective.

To Get Swift Action in a Court Case When You Encounter Constant Delays

A sink or washbasin with a plug

During the full moon

* Put in the plug and turn on the cold tap until the sink is almost full, saying, *Flow fast away, remove all delays. Clear away fast, so this case will not forever last.*

* Take out the plug and let the water go down the drain until the sink is almost empty. Then put the plug back in and fill the basin three-quarters full, repeating the spell. Then fill the sink half-full, then a quarter-full, repeating the spell words and actions.

* Finally, leave the tap running with the plug out, saying, *Flowing, moving, delays cleared. Good results near.* Gradually turn off the tap.

If You Need a Fast Official Decision or Permission and You Have Been Caught Up in Bureaucratic Red Tape

YOU WILL NEED

A pot of honey/treacle/maple syrup with a
lid * A spoon * A pancake/waffle

TIMING

When time is running out

THE SPELL

* Stir the honey with the spoon, saying, *Stuck in bureaucracy, nothing moving seems to be. Let's stir the pot. That should hasten decisions a lot.*

* Put a little honey on the pancake and eat it, saying, *Take a bite, make all right. Speed up the decision, end the imprecision. Now.*

* Put the lid back on the honey, saying, *Stuck in your bureaucracy, holding up people, but no longer me.*

To Find the Right Legal Representation if Your Current Lawyer is Not Acting Effectively on Your Behalf

YOU WILL NEED

Two sandalwood incense sticks * A brown stone
or crystal * A chrysocolla or white stone

TIMING

Tuesday

THE SPELL

* Light the first incense stick behind the brown stone, saying, *No more shilly-shallying please, with extortionate fees. You're not delivering the goods, as you should.*

* With the incense stick, draw a smoke cross over the stone, extinguish the incense, safely tossing the stone out the window and saying, *Once you were hired, now you are fired, no longer desired.*

* Light the second incense stick, setting the blue or white crystal in front of it, and say, *I need a replacement, swiftly now, fast, sharp, and keen, with fees that are lean. Results I will see, bring the right lawyer now to me.*

* Draw a smoke checkmark over the crystal, and leave the incense to burn through.

To Successfully Fight a Compensation Claim When People are Lying or Trying to Discredit You

YOU WILL NEED

Scissors ∗ A piece of white paper
∗ A quill pen or a feather with sharpened point
∗ A blue ribbon ∗ Dried sage

TIMING

Thursday

THE SPELL

* Round the edges of the paper with the scissors, write, and say, *This is the unvarnished truth, these are the facts, simply, plain. Those who lie and misrepresent, here I name.*

* Draw a box in the center of the paper, naming all who are lying or being obstructive.

* When the ink is dry, roll the paper into a scroll, tying it with ribbon in three knots, and say, *One all lies and falsehood bind, two discrediting testimonies wind, three justice and compensation shall I find* [name amount you seek].

* Leave the scroll for three days. Then scatter sage on the scroll and burn the scroll to release the powers.

If a Neighbor or a Local Gang Is Threatening Your Family and the Police Won't Intervene

A rosemary or sage wreath made by binding long sprigs of rosemary with twine around a wire or raffia hoop (see drawing) ★ Two small round mirrors with hooks ★ A white cloth

TIMING

Tuesday

280

THE SPELL

* Hang the rosemary wreath facing your nasty neighbor's property or, if you're threatened by a gang, on an inside wall facing the front door.

* Say, *Fierce fiery rosemary, defend my home and boundaries for me. For though I have inadequate protection legally, from those who should be there to see, yet you protect me magically.*

* Polish each mirror counterclockwise with the cloth, saying, *Reflect back all harm and threat, that the police may take me seriously yet. Until then I call on your repelling force, to drive away predators with magical laws.*

* Hang a mirror on either side of the wreath and repolish the mirror monthly. When the rosemary fades, replace it for ongoing protection.

If You are Having Issues With Citizenship or Residency for Yourself, a Partner, or Your Children

YOU WILL NEED

A photo of yourself in the country in which you seek residency, on top of pictures of your partner or the children you wish to join you ∗ A bowl of soil, set on top of the photo(s). ∗ Your favorite seeds or small plants indigenous to where you wish to live ∗ A planter

TIMING

The crescent moon

THE SPELL

∗ Put your hands around the bowl, saying, *My roots here are deep, this life I/we wish to keep, in my/our adopted home, no more to seek or roam.*

∗ Plant the seeds or seedlings, saying, *May this residency come soon and smoothly to me/my family, permanently. That we may make this adopted world our own, say securely, this is home.*

∗ Cut the photo(s) into four pieces and bury them in the corners of the planter.

If You Have Been Sold a Faulty Expensive Item and You Aren't Receiving a Satisfactory Remedy

YOU WILL NEED

A blue candle ★ A sandalwood incense stick ★ A strong, sealable paper bag

TIMING

Thursday morning

THE SPELL

* Draw invisibly in the wax of the unlit candle with the index finger of your dominant hand, the name of the person/company swindling you, saying, *I ask only for my rights, established by law. So what are you stalling for?*

* Light the candle and the incense, and repeat the spell words.

* After 5 minutes, extinguish and crush the incense, extinguish the candle and when they're both cool, shred them and put them both in the bag, saying, *Return my money or* [name item] *replace. Your injustice I will no longer tolerate. Act now, I will not wait.*

* Seal the envelope, write the name of the person/company swindling you on the front, and stamp on it, saying, *Crushed is your infamy, I will persist. You won't get the better of me.*

If You Sense That a Judge
and/or an Arbitration Panel
is Biased Against You

283

YOU WILL NEED

A small bag of salt and bag of flour of equal weight ✶ Scales
with two pans ✶ A container large enough for dough figures

TIMING

The week before a hearing

THE SPELL

✳ Hold one bag in each hand and say, *Salt, cleanser be, clear this inequality, flour, balancer be, that adjudication may in my favor be.*

✳ Open the bag of salt, and fill a third of one pan with salt. Then balance it with an equal weight of flour.

✳ When balanced, say, *The bias was there, weighed against me. But now is replaced, with impartiality.*

✳ Add water to make dough figures for each member of the panel, using flour and salt from the pans. *Say, I take back my power, respectful you shall be, unbiased in judgment henceforth toward me.*

✳ Keep the figures in a container until after the next hearing.

To Protect Yourself in a Vicious Family Inheritance Dispute

YOU WILL NEED

Blue beads, buttons, and crystals—three for each person involved in the dispute, including yourself ⋆ Different-colored small cloth bags, one for each person involved in the dispute, including yourself ⋆ A large green bag

TIMING

When meeting family members

THE SPELL

※ Divide the beads, buttons, and crystals equally among the small bags, shaking each in turn, naming the person, and saying for each one, *Fairness without animosity, in spite of what you believe should or not be. We are one family, and shall preserve unity.*

※ Place all the bags in the large bag and close it, shaking it six times, and say, *Not what's yours or rightfully mine, against dissension we draw the line.*

※ Keep the bag with a family photo of happier times.

If You Are Being Unfairly Accused of a Crime, at Work or by a Jealous Partner, and You are Innocent

YOU WILL NEED

Nine hazelnuts * A blue cloth or scarf

TIMING

Thursday at dawn

THE SPELL

* Hold each nut in turn, saying, *I protest my innocence, I will not be blamed. I have done nothing wrong, nor am ashamed.*

* Knot the hazelnuts nine times in the cloth, saying, *I gather my innocence, you are wrong to accuse. You stand there judgmental, I have so much to lose. I demand you believe me, I will clear my name. You who accuse me, slander and defame.*

* Undo the scarf and throw the nuts into any fast-flowing water, saying, *Here is my evidence, here my proof. Waters, carry to my accusers, the unvarnished truth.*

If a Relative or Friend is Imprisoned Overseas Under a Repressive Regime

YOU WILL NEED

The name of the relative, written on white paper in
blue ink ★ A small padlock and key, or a padlock
charm ★ A small lidded box ★ Ground nutmeg

TIMING

While you are awaiting news

THE SPELL

* Put the paper with the name written on it and the padlock and key in the box, and cover them with nutmeg, saying, *Sachiel, archangel of justice, who breaks through all chains, free* [Name] *from this unjust restraint. Sachiel, wise one, I ask home s/he be sent.*

* Open the box and leave it open for 24 hours, saying, *Open the door,* [Name] *to us restore.*

* Wash the padlock and key, and leave them close to the front door, holding them each morning, sending prayers that your loved one is being well-treated, and saying, *Open the door,* [Name] *to us restore.*

If You are Owed Money by a Big Organization or the Government and They Won't Pay Up

YOU WILL NEED

A computer

A large photo on the screen from the organization's website, showing representative personnel ∗ A smaller photo of yourself, next to the other photo on the screen

TIMING

Sunday

THE SPELL

∗ Point at the organization's picture and then yours, saying, *You are big, I am small, you would say, I've no chance at all. Of getting what you owe to me, but justice says that cannot be.*

∗ Reduce the size of the organization picture and increase the size of yours, saying, *You're not so big, I'm not so small. David made Goliath fall. Pay at once what you do owe. I shall not rest until it is so.*

∗ Keep reducing the size of their image and increasing the size of yours until theirs is tiny and your picture is large. Then place your photo on top of theirs, completely obscuring theirs.

∗ Find a picture of David and Goliath to use as your screen saver.

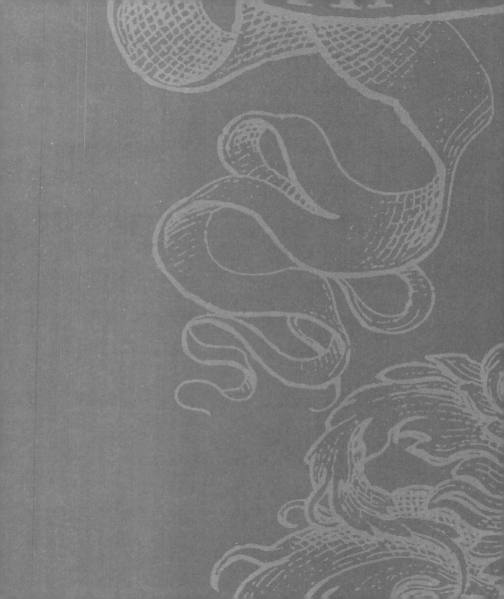

CHAPTER 17

Protecting Children FROM Harm AND Fear

Children are vulnerable to harm in our increasingly fast-paced and hazardous world. Kids face dangers from traffic, accidents at home, mercifully rare predators, and possibly getting lost in airports or shopping malls, no matter how carefully we watch them. Divorce and custody arrangements between parents, if there is bitterness, can cause children distress, especially if one of the parents is using the children as weapons in the domestic dispute. School days, too, supposedly the happiest days of your life, can bring uncertainty, teasing, and bullying of sensitive children or those who are different in some way. In spite of guidelines, schools are not always accepting of problems or alert to or prepared to deal with them.

Spells relating to children are especially effective because it would seem that parents have a telepathic bond with their children, and many of the spells can be shared with the child if the child is old enough. In other cases, a favorite toy or item can be empowered to carry the carry the defense of the child when s/he's away from home.

Though most of my spells here are directed to a single child, you can easily adapt them all if you have other children who would benefit from them.

To Protect an Unborn Child During Pregnancy and Create a Bond

Note: Either parent or both of you can do this.

YOU WILL NEED

Special music you play when sitting quietly ✳ Chamomile
or lavender essential oil ✳ A small round pink or
blue chalcedony or a rose quartz crystal

TIMING

In the evening

THE SPELL

* Play your special music.

* Anoint the center of your brow, your womb, or your inner wrist points with a drop of oil, to connect with the unborn child, saying, *Be safe within this sanctuary. Grow strong and healthy, until you be, safe in my/ your parents' arms. For now rest, sheltered from all harm.*

* Gently massage your womb with the crystal, repeating the spell words.

* Take the crystal, the oil, and the music into labor.

* Afterward, gently massage the baby with the crystal while playing your special music to soothe him/her, anointing your brow with the oil before doing this.

To Protect an Unborn Child if There Have Previously Been Miscarriages or Birth Trauma

YOU WILL NEED

A tiny doll ★ A white silk scarf ★ A white silk ribbon ★ A basket filled with dried rose petals

TIMING

When you conceive

THE SPELL

* Tie the doll securely in the scarf with the ribbon in nine knots, saying, *For nine months through, I will hold you, secure inside, safely abide. Rest easily, until strong and healthy, with me you be.*

* Place the scarf so it is resting in the basket with the rose petals. Scatter some petals on top, saying, *Remain safe, for full term. Until then I yearn, to have you in my arms, free from all harm. Angels guard and guide, that this beloved child, may grow secure inside.*

* When you are near your due date, untie the doll, putting her in the baby's room, and scattering the petals outdoors.

For an Easy and Safe Delivery

YOU WILL NEED

Two trailing green plants, one large and one small

TIMING

Toward the end of pregnancy

THE SPELL

* Tie a frond from the large plant to the small plant and another from the small plant to the larger one, saying, *Our hearts and souls still are one, and when into the world you come, gently, easily, I will hold you lovingly. Protecting you, your whole life through.*

* As labor begins or you are admitted for a C-section, carefully separate the fronds, saying, *As the new world you soon shall see, gently, easily, I hold you lovingly. Protecting you, beloved child, your whole life through.*

* When you both come home, set both plants closely in the same soil, plus a plant for your partner and any siblings, so the plants can grow together naturally.

To Protect an Infant in the First Months of Life

YOU WILL NEED

A small amber or coral bracelet ★ A white
candle ★ Sufficient pearls to fill a glass jar

TIMING

Each day after birth or homecoming

THE SPELL

* Place the bracelet in front of the candle.

* Each day light the candle, adding a pearl to the empty jar, saying,
  *Each day is a special day, since you came to earth, blessed by the angels
  who guard you after birth. Keeping from you all danger and distress,
  in these pearls my love also protects you, I vow no less.*

* Blow out the candle.

* Continue each day in exactly the same way until the jar is full,
  replacing the candle when necessary.

* Keep the jar of pearls high in the baby's room, hanging the bracelet
  on the wall until s/he is old enough to wear it.

To Protect a Child With Special Needs or a Disability from Teasing or Exclusion from Activities

YOU WILL NEED

Any beautiful asymmetrical crystal ✳ A bowl of water ✳ A white or silver scarf

TIMING

During the full moon when bright

THE SPELL

✳ Sit outdoors in moonlight, placing the crystal in the water.

✳ Splash the water on the ground, saying, *Mother Moon, uniqueness is your blessing, allow my child to reveal new talents without ceasing. That all may see his/her potential shining through, so through life, s/he is valued for what s/he is and not what s/he can do.*

✳ Leave the crystal in the water overnight.

✳ The next morning, dry the crystal with the scarf, saying, *Protected, enclosed would I keep you, that none may tease or disregard. Yet I know, I must let you go, but Mother Moon and I will you always guard, if life ever becomes too hard.*

✳ Bless the crystal at milestone points in the child's life.

To Prevent a Young Child from Getting Lost or Being Abducted

A photo of your child alone　✳　A photo of you and your child together　✳　Six tea lights or small white candles

Friday

* Place the two photos between a row of the tea lights.

* Light the candle nearest to your child's picture, saying, *One for love, angels above, keep my child safe with me.*

* Light the second candle, saying, *Two for love* and adding the rest of the spell words.

* Continue through candles 3, 4, and 5.

* Light candle 6, saying, *Six for love, angels above. Make this path of light, secure and always endure, by day and night.*

* Leave the candles to burn through. Whenever you and your child are out together, picture the link of light preventing him/her from straying or being abducted. Keep the photos in a wallet with you or on your smartphone.

To Protect a Child While Traveling

YOU WILL NEED

Two bar magnets

Anything in the color turquoise that can be attached
or given to the child, such as a turquoise button, a turquoise
badge, or a turquoise bracelet * A small piece of
turquoise cloth * A turquoise or blue purse or small bag

TIMING

A day or two before travel

THE SPELL

* Place the magnets, poles repelling, one on either side of the turquoise item, saying, *I link with you magnetically, I join you to me energetically. I protect you while traveling magically. Whether we travel together or apart, I hold you safe within my heart.*

* Hold the magnets above the turquoise item, poles attracting, so they jump together.

* Wrap the magnets, still together, in the cloth, putting them and the item in the bag.

* Before travel, take out the turquoise item and attach/give it to the child, saying the spell words in your mind.

To Help a Child with Disorders, Such as Autism or Asperger's Syndrome, to Adapt to the World

298

YOU WILL NEED

A square, made up of eight crystals in all, which include either four lapis lazuli and four amethyst crystals or four blue and four purple glass nuggets or beads placed alternately throughout the square ★ A triangle of blue candles around the square of crystals ★ A picture of the child in the center of the square ★ A key on top of the picture

TIMING

A quiet time and place

THE SPELL

✳ Touch each of the crystals, first counterclockwise fast, then slowly clockwise, saying, *Understanding the way life works, following the patterns the fast world talks.*

✳ Light the candles slowly, clockwise, saying, *But you have much to teach us too, to value order pure and true.*

✳ Blow out the candles.

✳ Pick up and hold the key, saying, *The key to unlocking life's doors, to find the way to our world from yours. Yet not losing your unique identity, but teaching us priorities.*

✳ Keep the key in a quiet place, surrounded by the crystal square.

To Support a Child Going to Kindergarten or School for the First Time

YOU WILL NEED

A small toy or item, regularly carried by the child

TIMING

A week before the child begins school

THE SPELL

* Touch your heart and then the item, saying, *I cannot come with you all the way, but you are in my heart every second you are away. May your days be joyous, all you meet be kind. May new adventures and good friends you find.*

* Hug the item and repeat the spell words. When the child is asleep, briefly touch the child's heart with it, saying the spell words in your mind.

* When the child is ready to leave for school, hold the item to your heart and hug the child with the item between you, before giving it to the child, saying in your mind the same spell words.

For a Child Who Has No Friends

YOU WILL NEED

Modeling clay ★ Party streamers
or brightly colored ribbons

TIMING

Before the beginning of the school week

THE SPELL

* Make a series of five clay figures, including one for your child.

* Hold in your hands your child's figure and one of the others, saying,
  *One beloved child, no longer playing alone. I call a friend and now
  s/he has one.* Join the two figures together with their hands.

* Continue adding the figures, saying, *One beloved child, no longer playing
  alone. I call another friend to you, now there are two.*

* Adapt the rhyme as you add the rest of the figures . . . *I call another
  friend to make you happy, now there are three . . .* finally . . . *and that is
  even more, now there are four.*

* Join all the hands in a circle and bind them together with party
  streamers or ribbons.

To Help a Child Deal with Divorce or Separation

Three pictures—one with the child and her/his mother, one with the child and her/his father, and a central one of everyone ✳ One of the child's treasured possessions ✳ A duplicate of the child's treasured possession the child possesses ✳ A blue candle behind each of the outer pictures

TIMING

When the decision is made to separate from the child's other parent

THE SPELL

* Light the outer candles, saying for each one, *We your parents are both here for you, you mustn't think you have to choose. An extra home, a brand-new room, everything will be in twos.*

* Place the child's original treasured possession on the left photo and the duplicate of the child's treasured possession on the right photo.

* Leave the candles to burn.

* When the child goes to the other parent's home, light the candle behind that parent's picture, saying, *This candle and my care will shine for you, as special times in your new home you share, the whole time through.*

* Give the child the duplicate treasure to keep.

To Protect a Child Who is Unwilling to Go On Custody Visits to the Other Parent

YOU WILL NEED

A picture of the whole family together ∗ A green pen
∗ A scarf you often wear ∗ A rose-scented candle

TIMING

A day or two before a planned visit

THE SPELL

∗ On the back of the picture, write in green pen the name of your
  ex and the words, KIND BE, TREAD GENTLY, ACT PATIENTLY. TAKE CARE
  OF [name child] FOR ME. THIS IS NOT ABOUT POWER, BUT EVERY HOUR
  WITH YOU, DEVOTED SHALL YOU BE, FOR STILL WE ARE FAMILY.
  Fold the picture and place it inside the scarf.

∗ Trace invisibly the same words on the unlit candle.

∗ Light the candle. Set the scarf containing the folded picture near
  the candle, until the candle burns through.

∗ Before the visit, give your child the scarf, repeating the spell words
  in your mind.

∗ Light another candle behind the picture after the child leaves
  and every evening while s/he is away.

To Assist a Child with Parental Rejection if One Parent Refuses to Maintain Contact After a Divorce

A large white candle with three wicks (additional wicks for extra children) ✳ Three (or more) separate smaller white candles, set around the large one— one for you, your ex, and each of your children.

TIMING

Any Friday evening if the child(ren) is/are sad

THE SPELL

✳ Light the wicks on the big candle, saying, *Once we were in unity, now, Beloved Child(ren) you and me. But still the family light will glow, this I believe and this I know.*

✳ Light separate candles for you and your child(ren) and one for the absent partner.

✳ Blow out the absent parent candle, relighting it from each of the large candle's wicks, and say, *We call you to contact us, when the time is right. Until then, we burn the family light.*

✳ Leave all the candles to burn through.

To Enable a Child to Settle Down After a Major Move Here or Overseas

YOU WILL NEED

A green jade crystal or a moss agate ★ Something
your child treasures or a special picture of
him/her ★ A plant growing in your old home

TIMING

Two weeks before you move

THE SPELL

* Place the crystal with something your child treasures or by a special picture of him/her, saying, *Take with you happy memories, of your life here and more to be. You may move far but happily, and your new home will soon become familiar territory.*

* On week 2 bury the crystal, marking it in the earth or a planter, and leave it until you move. Wash it, repeating the spell words.

* If you can't take the same plant with you, buy another one, reburying the crystal in a planter in your new home.

* After a week, rewash the crystal and keep it with the child's picture or treasures.

To Help a Child When There is Family Bereavement

A small table containing mementos and photos of
the deceased person and a vase of the deceased
person's favorite flowers * A white candle

In the days after the funeral

* As the child looks at or holds the items, light the candle, saying,
  Though [Name] *from this world has gone, the memory and their kindness
  linger on. Recalling special times we shared, when we talk of* [Name],
  their love is there.

* Leave the candle to burn through. When the flowers die, take them
  with the child to a place you were all happy and scatter the petals,
  saying, *We send these flowers to the sky. Like our love for* [Name],
  they fly and never die.

* Buy flowers of exactly the same kind to put on the memory table and
  keep repeating the scattering and replacing every time the flowers die.

To Protect a Child from Fear of the Dark and Nightmares

Note: If the child is very young, say the spell as the child sleeps and put the angel high, switching on the lamp when you hear the little one stirring and repeating the spell words.

YOU WILL NEED

A small white or opalite angel ✴ A children's battery-powered lamp, radiating colored spheres, stars, or rainbows

TIMING

Before sleep

THE SPELL

✴ Let the child hold the angel. Say, *Angel Muriel, on her magick carpet is protecting you, wrapped safe in her rainbow, the whole night through. And if you wake, nasty dreams and scary darkness away she will take.*

✴ Switch on the lamp and hold the angel so the beams are all around her, repeating the spell words.

✴ Put the angel by the bedside and show the child how to operate the lamp's safety switch, calling for Muriel.

To Banish Ghosts and Spirits from a Psychic Child Who is Frightened of Them

YOU WILL NEED

A white candle ✳ Rose essential oil,
mixed with virgin olive oil

TIMING

*When the child is
not in the house*

THE SPELL

✳ Go into the child's bedroom and any other areas where
the child sees spirits carrying the lighted white candle.

✳ Stand in the center of each room, facing each direction in turn,
saying, *Shapes and visions of other places, ancestors from bygone ages,
my child can see you, knows you're there. Remain invisible, silent,
and remove his/her fear.*

✳ Afterwards extinguish the candle, putting it outside the front door.

✳ Visit each room again, anointing with the oil over lintels of doors
and around door- and windowframes with the index finger of
your dominant hand the glyph of Archangel Uriel (see drawing),
protective archangel with his fiery torch, repeating the spell words.

✳ Use the remaining oil in a diffuser.

To Overcome Jealousy Against a New Baby or Siblings

YOU WILL NEED

Three or four peacock feathers with a clear eye (not at all unlucky)
in a vase in the den ★ A vase of pink roses in the same room

TIMING

When the children are not present

THE SPELL

* Touch each eye in turn, saying, *Jealousy begone from here. All shall be loving, all are dear.*

* Carry the vase of feathers through each room in turn, repeating the spell words, then carry the peacock feathers out the front door.

* Carry the vase of roses through each room in turn, saying, *Love there is enough to share* [name jealous child(ren)], *for one another we must care. I banish jealousy in the roses' name. We shall love one another, equally the same.*

* Replace the roses whenever they fade. Give the peacock feathers to charity or someone who will cherish them.

To Help a Child Adjust to a New Step-Parent if You are the Step-Parent

Red thread * A fairy tale, written on paper, that
you have created about a wonderful step-parent and
loving stepchildren * A toy or model dragon
* A modeling clay figure of each stepchild, plus one
of you wearing a crown and/or brandishing a sword

TIMING

Before a visit

THE SPELL

* Tie up the story and put the dragon on top, saying, *The wicked dragon tried to stop the happily ever after, this cannot be. My stepchild(ren) and I will live if not in bliss, in reasonable harmony.*

* Remove the dragon, and tie him up.

* Free the story and put the figures on top, saying, *The Fairy Queen/the Valiant Sword rescued the grateful children. Well, maybe they weren't that impressed, but almost a happy conclusion.*

* Put the dragon in the dark, keeping the figures and the story in sunshine.

To Rescue a Child Who is Always Being Set Up as the Fall Guy

YOU WILL NEED

Ten feathers in a pouch ★ A photo of your child

TIMING

Saturday

THE SPELL

* Find a straight long path and walk along it slowly, saying, [Name], *Tread softly and warily, don't stand in the firing line. Act and speak cautiously, take your time. Don't let others pull your strings, they set you up for all kinds of things. Smiling innocently, while you the fall guy are made to be. And so you speak impulsively and get the blame. Stop their game.*

* Drop each feather at regular intervals, saying the same spell words for each one until all are gone except one.

* Attach that one to the back of a photo of your child, repeating the words.

To Protect a Child (or Children) from Being Fed Lies About You or Being Constantly Bribed by the Custodial Parent

YOU WILL NEED

A blue drawstring bag, containing any four of the following: nutmeg; dried leaves from oak, ash, redwood, or another tall strong tree in your region; thyme; valerian; sandalwood; or sage

TIMING

When contact is rejected

THE SPELL

* Open the bag and whisper over it, *Beloved child(ren), what you are told about me is untrue. I long to share the truth with you. I never did betray you, nor willingly leave* [or name unfair accusation]. *I, your mother/father daily for you grieve.*

* Hang the bag indoors. Every Friday reopen the bag, whispering again the spell words.

* Renew the contents every month and scatter the old ones to the wind, saying, *May the truth become clear to see, and you turn again to me. Until then, I send you love and harmony.*

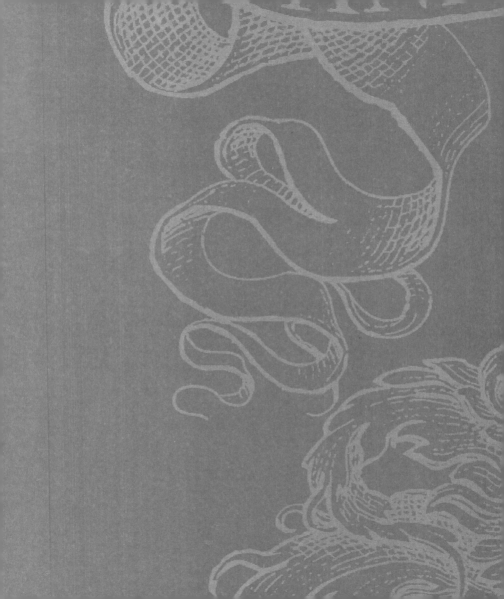

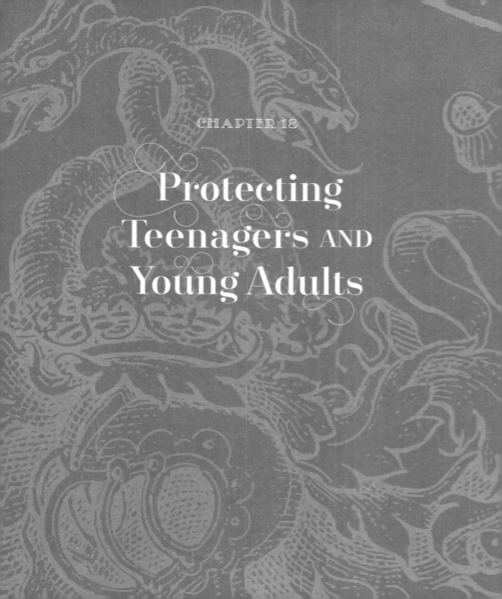

CHAPTER 18

Protecting Teenagers AND Young Adults

As children become teenagers and young adults, their growing desire for independence is compounded by parental worries about their falling into the wrong company and growing up before they are emotionally ready. Life holds many temptations for the young—recreational drugs, alcohol, opportunities to party all night and sleep all day, and the danger of committing petty crime to appear cool to friends without considering the consequences.

We can offer all the advice in the world and call upon counseling services (where available and this can vary hugely), but oftentimes the young minds in grown-up bodies do not listen. Spells can put safeguards around our vulnerable young people as they grow into adulthood. You will find other spells for and about teenagers throughout this book, especially in the chapters on bullying online (chapter 7) and fears and phobias (chapter 10). While I do not believe in interfering magically or actually with free will, if we see a young person we love heading toward serious danger, I believe we have the right to intervene magically, especially if earthly efforts are meeting a brick wall. But use your judgment if you disagree with this.

When Your Teenager is Determined to Move in with the Other Parent You Believe Won't Offer Safe Care

YOU WILL NEED

A ransom note written by you as if from the teenager, listing demands and threats ✳ A photo of the teenager, wrapped in a silk scarf

TIMING

After a confrontation

THE SPELL

✳ Hold the note, saying, *I'm no sheriff or marshal of law, but I won't be held captive by you* [Name]. *What do you take me for?*

✳ Rip up the note, unwrap the photo, and say, *Nice and cushy, you have been, pampered in finest silk. But I tell you, gal/young man, me you'll no longer milk.*

✳ Shake the photo, saying, *You've led me in a merry dance. Shape up now or take your chance.*

✳ When your teenager comes home, say in your mind, *I've spelled it out magically, now I'll say it actually.*

✳ State *your* terms loud and clear.

If Your Teenager or Young Adult is Rapidly Becoming Drawn Into the World of Drugs

YOU WILL NEED

A heatproof tray on which you have
traced invisibly a banishing pentagram
(see drawing) ★ Five incense cones
on the heatproof tray, one on
each point of the invisibly drawn
pentagram ★ A battery-powered fan

BANISHING
PENTAGRAM

TIMING

Wednesday

THE SPELL

* Light each of the incense cones in the order 1–5 above, saying for each one, *You who lead my child into temptation, to pushers and addicts with no hesitation, I banish you all who tempt and lure, your presence in his/her life I shall not endure.*

* When the incense cones are burned and the ash is cool, take the tray outdoors and, using a battery-powered fan, scatter the ash, saying, *Blow away, go away, away must you stay. The price on his/her life is too high to pay.*

* Scrub the tray clean.

If Your Teenager or Young Adult is Regularly Drinking to Excess and Putting Him/Herself in Danger

317

YOU WILL NEED

A small bottle of flavored alcohol or sweet wine ★ Vinegar ★ Lemon juice ★ Bitter aloes powder (optional)

TIMING

When your child has come home drunk

THE SPELL

* Pour away the alcohol and replace it with half vinegar and half lemon juice, adding a pinch of bitter aloes powder, if desired. Say, *Not so sweet, not so nice, when next you drink, it won't taste right.*

* Pour that mix away and keep making the mix in the bottle, adding more and more water and leaving out the aloes until, eventually, you are just adding clear water. Say, *Money poured down the drain, if you seek pleasure from booze, it will be in vain. Each time you drink to excess, the pleasure will get less and less.*

* Pour away the water and throw away the bottle.

If Your Teenager or Young Adult
is Out of Control

318

YOU WILL NEED

Children's modeling clay, green and red ★ A few small
clear crystals or glass nuggets ★ Greenery

TIMING

When you can't cope any more

THE SPELL

* Make two small clay figures, one in gentle green with a smile and the other bright red with a snarl.

* Say, as you hold the red one, *Violent, wild, are you my child? A changeling you must be, destroying, fighting, keeping bad company.*

* Hold the green figure, saying, *All must be as it was before. I don't want a saint, but can stand this no more.*

* Roll both figures together. From them create a new figure, pressing into it the crystals, and say, *Shine your true kind self in my life again. So my belief in you will not be in vain.*

* Leave this figure wrapped in greenery in a sunny green outdoor place until it crumbles.

To Get Another Chance if Your Teenager or Young Adult Has Broken the Law and is in Danger of Going to Prison

YOU WILL NEED

Toy bricks, including a door formed from the bricks * A bag of dried lavender

TIMING

A week before the court hearing

THE SPELL

* Build a wall of toy bricks around the bag of lavender, including the closed door, saying, *You are not wicked, only easily misled. You have learned your lesson. May you be spared prison, and given a chance to turn life around instead.*

* Open the toy-brick door and take down the wall, saying, *Open the door, I take down the wall, so all need not fall.*

* Scatter the lavender outdoors, saying, *Life's not a game, you've made a mistake. But if given this chance, a good life you'll make.*

* Repeat the ritual nightly until the case is heard in court. On the last night, keep the lavender bag intact and take it to the hearing.

If Your Teenager or Young Adult Has Become a Recluse and Stays Locked Away from the World

YOU WILL NEED

Four lavender incense sticks, set in a square around a picture of the child in happier days ★ A glass of water with a clear quartz crystal in it, set on top of the picture

TIMING

Sunday

THE SPELL

* Light the incense clockwise, saying, *Break down the prison, made from your thoughts. Bring down the barriers, behind which you are caught.*

* Put the burned cool incense in a box, remove the crystal from the water, and use the crystal water in drinks for the recluse, saying, *Open the door, hide no more.*

* Repeat the spell each day for a week, making fresh crystal water, and on day 7 scatter the accumulated ash beyond the boundaries of the home, saying, *The world waits on the other side of the door. Hide no more.*

If Your Teen or Young Adult
Has Dropped Out of School
or College and Won't Get a Job

321

YOU WILL NEED

A bottle of carbonated lemonade or a bottle
of sparkling water * A red pen

TIMING

Late waxing or full moon

THE SPELL

* Write his/her name on the label on the bottle, saying, *Motivate,
  life won't wait. Work, travel, study, whatever you will. But get off your
  backside, don't wait until it's too late.*

* Shake the bottle outdoors and take off the cap so it sprays everywhere.
  Say, *So life isn't fair, I don't really care. Get out there. Earn, learn, explore
  other lands. But do something now. Seize life with both hands.*

* Offer your child a bottle of carbonated water or a drink, having shaken
  it well beforehand, along with a lot of brochures, course choices, etc.

If Your Teenager is Stealing from You or You Suspect Her/Him of Shoplifting

YOU WILL NEED

Two incense sticks, one dragon's blood and one pine, in two holders ★ A modeling clay figure with long arms, with twelve coins circled around it ★ A bowl of soil or sand

TIMING

During the waning moon

THE SPELL

* Light the dragon's blood incense stick and make smoke crosses in the air over, first, the figure, then counterclockwise over each coin, saying, *Not yours, mine, or stolen I find. Keep your thieving hands to yourself, and leave unpaid goods on the shelf.*

* Plunge the dragon's blood incense stick, lighted side down, into the sand.

* Light the pine incense stick and make circles over the figure and coins clockwise, saying, *Temptation begone, your thieving is done. Never in future reach out to steal, or your crimes I will reveal to all. Your call.*

* Reduce the length of the arms.

If Your Teenager Has Special Needs and You Can't Get Official Help for Placement in an Independent Living Home

YOU WILL NEED

A box of coins of any denomination or currency, tied with three knots of blue thread ∗ A sharp knife ∗ A plastic tube, open at one end ∗ Official communications regarding the placement

TIMING

Thursday

THE SPELL

∗ Shake the box three times, saying, *Officialdom, I'm done with you, hanging on to resources, that to my child are due.*

∗ Cut the knots, saying *Free us from this pointless dance. Fund the future, and give him/her a chance.*

∗ Spill the coins out and, one by one, put them in the tube, shaking it and saying, *My child deserves this break in life, so pay up now and end this strife.*

∗ Scatter the contents of the tube from a height, then collect the money and put that in the open box on top of official communication.

If Your Teenager is Obsessively in Love and Giving Everything Up to Move in with a User and Loser

YOU WILL NEED

A black crayon or marker ★ White paper ★ Two blue crystals or glass beads, each tangled separately in blue thread ★ Scissors

TIMING

A sunny day

THE SPELL

* With the black crayon, draw a pair of eyes on the paper and set a crystal in the center of each, saying, [name child], *Open your eyes, start to be wise. In love you are blind, but only sorrow in this obsession you'll find.*

* Cut off the threads and wash the crystals under running water, saying, *Open your eyes, S/he's telling you lies. You're blinkered with desire, but you're playing with fire. Just wait, it's not too late.*

* Hide the eyes with the dried crystals on top of them under the teenager's carpet or behind his/her bedroom furniture.

If Your Teen or Young Adult is Depressed and Won't Accept Help

YOU WILL NEED

A long, thin, white cloth ★ A very small quantity of washable black paint or ink, dissolved in water ★ Stain remover or whitener

TIMING

Sunday morning

THE SPELL

* Dip the cloth in the ink/paint, saying, *All seems dark,* [Name], *you have lost your spark. Everything seems gray, from life and we who love you, you have turned right away.*

* Put the cloth in the washing machine with some stain remover and whitener, saying, *Wash sorrow away. Reach out and know, the darkness can go. Restored shall be the light of day. Hold my hand, and I will try, your pain to understand, and guide your way.*

* Keep washing until the cloth is white again and hang it from a tree in sunlight. Repeat the spell monthly, replacing the old cloth on the tree.

CHAPTER 19

Spells for Teenagers and Young Adults to Cast to Deal with the Stresses, Complexities, and Problems of Modern Life

This chapter is closely linked to the previous chapter. However, it is planned so that teenagers and young adults can cast their own spells from their perspective. These spells will offer them protection from the increasing pressures of the modern world and worries about the future, love when no one approves, exclusion by peers, and pressure from parents to fit into *their* lifestyles and follow *their* dreams.

When parents are divorced, some young people find themselves in the role of go-between or buffer in their parents' marital disharmony or trapped in a restrictive environment where gender issues and the clash between a traditional and a modern culture can cause distress.

The spells in the previous chapter can also be easily adapted if, for example, a teenager or young adult is worried about his/her own spiraling, out-of-control alcohol issues, or can't get help for their special needs to become independent. Indeed, there are spells in the previous chapter, for example, about teenage love and career choices that mirror issues in this chapter, but are sometimes seen from a very different perspective.

If You Have a Seemingly Impossible Dream and Everyone Laughs or Opposes You

YOU WILL NEED

A children's bubble wand ✳ Bubble mix

TIMING

Any morning in an open space

THE SPELL

✳ Begin to blow bubbles slowly, saying, *This is my dream* [name it]. *Others may laugh and despise, but I will achieve it, my dream, however unlikely it may seem, to rise as high as the skies.*

✳ Keep blowing bubbles faster, saying, *Mock all you choose, my dream I'll not lose.*

✳ When all the bubble mix is gone, shake the container upside down, saying, *Like bubbles in the skies, I'll prove myself to all eyes, some bits of my dream, like bubbles, may fall, but I will win all. And so I call my dream.*

If Other Students at School or College are Ganging Up on You Because You are Different

Pictures of the ringleaders on your computer screen,
drawn from social media ⋆ A brown stone for each
ringleader ⋆ A pot of compost or soil ⋆ A sharp stick

TIMING

Wednesday

THE SPELL

* Point to the first picture on the left, saying, *Bully girl/boy, smirking in a row, ganging up together, off one goes.*

* Delete the picture from the screen. Drop the stone in the compost, poking it down with the stick.

* Continue the spell until only one face is left on the screen. Say, *One nasty bully boy/girl, left all alone. Feel the pain I feel. Your weakness I reveal, now you've lost everyone.*

* Delete the final picture and bury the last stone, substituting a happy picture of yourself. Dump the contents of the pot.

If You are Experiencing Prejudice in a Traditional Environment Over Transgender Issues or Same-Sex Relationships

YOU WILL NEED

A flashlight and a path, if possible lit by solar lights or small lamps ✳ Sandalwood or rose potpourri in a small bag worn over your shoulder

TIMING

After dark (in a safe place)

THE SPELL

✳ Switch on your flashlight, follow the path, and say, *I am what I am, I value what I am. I will follow life, according to my plan.*

✳ Scattering potpourri to either side as you walk, say, *Soften their minds, make them more kind. That their prejudice will cease, I seek not their blessing, only peace. Until then keep me safe, from all opposition. I don't ask you to like me, just accept my decisions.*

✳ When you reach the end, scatter any remaining potpourri, turn around, and walk home in silence.

If You Can't Find a Boyfriend or Girlfriend and Everyone Else Has One

YOU WILL NEED

A bowl, large enough to fit a fully submerged
small mirror, filled with water ★ Six silver candles
★ A small makeup or hand mirror ★ A white cloth

TIMING

*During the full moon (if it is cloudy,
light a semicircle of silver candles indoors)*

THE SPELL

❋ Hold the mirror horizontally with your dominant hand just under
the surface of running water to catch the moon or candlelight in it.

❋ Gaze into the watery mirror, saying, *I take within me the radiance of
the moon, that true love will come and find me soon.*

❋ Splash water drops onto your face, repeating the spell words.

❋ Lift the mirror, pressing your lips against the damp mirror.

❋ Finally wipe the mirror counterclockwise with the cloth until it's dry.
Pour the water on the ground, blowing out the candles.

❋ Take the mirror with you before you go on a potential date,
looking into it and repeating the spell words.

If Your Parents Can't Afford Your Dream Dress for the Prom

YOU WILL NEED

A mirror, in which small tea lights or candles are shining) ∗ A children's magick wand ∗ A pumpkin

TIMING

After dark

THE SPELL

∗ Stand in front of the mirror, waving your wand in alternate directions and saying, *Magick Mirror on the wall, I'm desperate for a prom dress and so on you I call. Fairy Godmother, you dressed Cinderella for the ball, can't you help me at all?*

∗ Blow softly into each light, saying, *My folks really have done their best, so on you my hopes do rest. Any legal way at all, please dress me for this once-in-a-lifetime, wonderful ball.*

∗ Lift the pumpkin to the mirror, saying, *Send to me unexpectedly, the right dress and opportunity. And I'll be good, I really could, magick, work for me, one, two, three.*

∗ Blow out the candles fast.

∗ Look for an unexpected dress offer everywhere.

∗ Make a pumpkin pie for your parents.

If No One Understands You

A ball

During the crescent moon

* Bounce the ball rhythmically against a wall, saying, *I really tried, not to hide, what I am inside. But you don't get me, and I can't be what you want to see. Understand me.*

* Catch the ball, then throw and catch it up and down, saying, *A new ball game, In my own name, listen to what I really say, value me for who I am. Then I can, try to play, your game too. But you must understand, I am not you.*

* Throw the ball high, catch it, then kick the ball as far as you can, saying, *Understand me.*

334

If You are in Love and Your Parents Oppose the Relationship

Two identical rose quartz hearts or round crystals
★ A pink heart, cut from silk ★ Two pink candles
★ Rose petals or rose potpourri ★ Two small green bags

TIMING

Friday, during the waxing moon

THE SPELL

* Place the crystals side by side on the silk heart. Place the candles on either side of the heart.

* Scatter a heart shape of petals around the silk heart, light the candles, and say, *Within this heart of flowers, love shall eternally be ours. Though we are young, We know our minds. We ask the world to be kind. Don't try to split us apart. We know our hearts.*

* Blow out the candles and scoop up a little of the potpourri to put in each bag with a rose quartz heart.

* Keep one bag each. Put the rest of the potpourri in a bowl in your bedroom.

If Your Parents Won't Give You Any Independence and Treat You Like a Child

YOU WILL NEED

An oversized modeling clay figure in a tiny cradle ✳ A single large creeping plant

TIMING

During the full moon

THE SPELL

✳ Lift the figure out of the cradle and say, *Mom, Dad, you cling to me too tightly, stifling me. Time to leave the cradle, space just to be.*

✳ Dig up the plant and divide the roots into two, the larger one for your parent(s) and the smaller one for yourself.

✳ Replant them in separate pots or in the earth some distance away from each other.

✳ Bury the cradle in the soil of your plant, setting your figure among the foliage so your plant will grow around it, saying, *Mom, Dad I still want you in my life naturally. But, first I must find out, whom I can be.*

✳ Tend both plants and when you are ready to move away from home, take your plant with you.

If Parents and Teachers are Pushing You Down a Career Path You Don't Want

YOU WILL NEED

A pointed stick * A sand tray or a sandbox
half-filled with sand * Sunflower seeds

TIMING

Monday

THE SPELL

* With the stick, draw two parallel lines in the sandbox, saying, *I don't necessarily want to be an astronaut, though, that would be cool, of course. But don't railroad me down this narrow track. Ability I may have, but enthusiasm I lack.*

* Rub out the two lines and scatter sunflower seeds in all directions across the sandbox, saying, *I must be free, to choose my own destiny. To test and try, not to let life pass me by. I must my own future make, and correct my own mistakes.*

* Plant the seeds in the soil and water well.

If Warring Parents Treat You as a Go-Between or a Pawn

YOU WILL NEED

A piece of red cord, strung horizontally between two hooks on the wall with a toy bell in the middle ★ A green cord

TIMING

Saturday

THE SPELL

* Ring the bell, saying, *From one to the other, from father to mother, whatever I say, whatever I do, the other will complain I'm favoring you.*

* Remove the red cord (the parental cord) from the hooks and take off the bell, saying, *I won't take sides, be your go-between. I'm quitting this scene. Won't play ball, answer your call, I'm done with it all.*

* Hang the bell, secured with three knots, to the green cord (your cord) and hang it vertically behind your door.

* Ring the bell as a reminder every time you know you will be asked to take sides and hang the parental cord far outside your home.

If Your Family Belongs to a Culture Where You are Socially Restricted and Stuck Between Worlds

YOU WILL NEED

Two beeswax candles, placed close together on a heatproof tray ✳ A narrow screwdriver or letter opener ✳ A scarf

TIMING

During the crescent moon

THE SPELL

✳ Before lighting, hold each candle, saying for the first one, *I love my traditions* and for the other *I long to share the new world.*

✳ Light both candles, saying, *Not two but one, makes up the sum. Let me explore a lifestyle new. My home and family I will not betray you.*

✳ When the wax has formed a pool, as it cools draw in the wax a figure representing yourself, wearing on one side traditional garments and on the other a more modern outfit. Say, *Two parts of me, in harmony. Don't make me choose, or we all will lose.*

✳ Cut out and keep your beeswax figure with your private things, wrapped in a scarf.

If You are Psychic and Have Premonitions of Disasters That Scare You

YOU WILL NEED

A telescope or binoculars ★ A heavy cloth or
a special case for the telescope/binoculars

TIMING

At sunset

THE SPELL

* Move the telescope/binoculars so that the lenses gradually become out of focus, saying, *What I cannot in the future change, I do not wish to see. Close this door, I don't want to know before, what is to be. If a disaster I can't prevent, I return this foreknowledge before it is sent.*

* Wrap the telescope/binoculars in heavy cloth or in the case.

* Repeat the spell weekly until you feel the powers diminishing. If you do get a feeling/picture starting to appear in your mind, visualize the out-of-focus telescope and repeat the spell words.

If Your Boy/Girlfriend Has Dumped You and Gone Off with Your Best Friend

YOU WILL NEED

Two toy snakes ✳ Lemon rind

TIMING

When you discover the betrayal

THE SPELL

✳ Intertwine the snakes so they are twisted around each other, saying, *Snakes in the grass, this wrong cannot pass. You both lied and betrayed me. Do you really think two snakes happy together can be?*

✳ Rub the snakes with the lemon rind, saying, *I curse you not, nor send you harm. But two snakes in love, ring every alarm.*

✳ Dump the snakes, still entwined, in tall grass or mud, and leave the lemon rind to dry out before throwing it away.

✳ Get out there and find someone worthy of you.

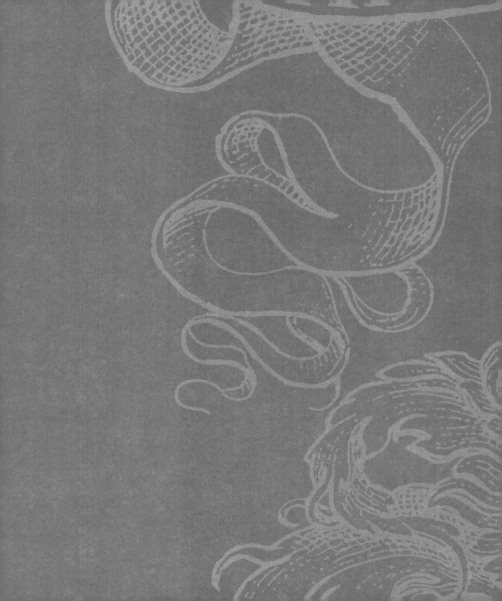

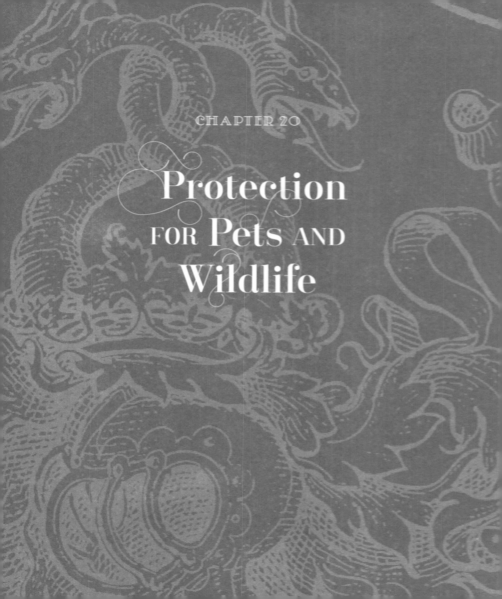

CHAPTER 20

Protection
FOR Pets AND
Wildlife

For many of us, pets, large and small, are an integral part of our family, so their health and well-being are very important to us. But in our modern, fast-paced, noisy world, there are many hazards that can befall them. Even in the age of microchips, pets, especially if they're valuable, are in danger of being stolen or simply wandering off, being suddenly frightened and lost.

The easiest way to protect your pets is by attaching an empowered crystal or medallion to their collar or bridle. In general, there are one or two situations in your daily life where you need specific protection for your pet. However, you can collect in a small box different empowered medallions or crystals to attach to a pet's collar or bridle for various situations where protection is needed. Turquoise is an all-purpose protection stone.

Wildlife, too, throughout the world is becoming increasingly endangered, with whole species being brought to the point of extinction through loss of habitat, polluted seas, or poaching, and this is a real problem for the legacy we leave future generations. So, too, are wild and exotic creatures still kept in unacceptable conditions in parts of the world or forced to perform for our entertainment, having been brutally trained.

We can't put it all right, but spells can offer protection to pets who are within our care and send healing energies to other creatures we know are in danger or are being ill treated.

A Four-Day Protection Spell to Keep Pets from Straying or Being Lured Away

YOU WILL NEED

Nine hairs from your pet and nine of yours,
tied with thread onto a metal tag with
the pet's name and contact details engraved
* A bottle of Dr. Bach's Cerato Flower Remedy™
or Five-Flower Rescue Remedy™

TIMING

Four nights, toward the end of the waning moon

THE SPELL

* Hold the tag in the darkness outdoors, saying, *May you* [Name] *not stray or be lured away. I bind you with my love by night and day. Beloved pet, safely with me stay.*

* Repeat the spell for the next three nights.

* On night 4, sprinkle a few drops of Cerato or Five-Flower Rescue Remedy in a circle around it. The next day attach it to the pet's collar or bridle. When the pet goes out next, sprinkle a little Cerato across the doorway.

A Turquoise Defense Spell for Horses and Their Riders, Stable Hands, and Trainers

A beeswax candle ∗ A small turquoise stone mounted
in a wire cradle through which a piece of wire is threaded
∗ Any product made from bee pollen or royal jelly

TIMING

Sunday

THE SPELL

346

∗ Light the beeswax candle and hold the turquoise stone to the candlelight, saying, *You are precious to me. Large you may be, but your vulnerability as well as nobility I can see. Protect against all who would harm or scare, from traffic, spectators, malice, and those who would snare. Guard those who ride, train, and care for horses also. Hariel, angel of horses, always be there.*

∗ Rub just a little of the pollen or jelly on the turquoise stone, repeating the spell words.

∗ Blow out the candle, wipe the turquoise, and attach it to the horse's bridle or the stable door.

∗ Wear a similarly empowered turquoise stone when you ride, during training, or while competing.

A Gentle Rose Quartz Protection Spell
for Timid or High-Strung Pets

A pink candle ✳ A collar ✳ A rose quartz mounted
in a wire cradle, and attached to the collar by a
piece of wire, in front of the candle ✳ Dried
chamomile (split a tea bag or two)

TIMING

Friday, the day of Archangel Ariel, who protects all creatures

THE SPELL

347

* Light the candle, saying, [name pet(s)], *I enfold you with the light of my love and of Ariel above. That you may walk unmolested and not afraid or facing danger, from other creatures or frightening strangers. And if you roam, safely return home, guided by love, and Ariel above.*

* Scatter a square of chamomile around the candle and the collar, repeating the spell words.

* Leave the candle to burn and attach the collar to the animal.

* Scoop up the chamomile, making a trail outside the animal flap/door. If you're using the crystal on a bridle, empower the crystal separately, by placing it outdoors in the moonlight overnight. Best results are achieved under a full moon.

If Your Pet Must Travel or Move Home Separately from You or Be Quarantined

YOU WILL NEED

Four banded or brown agates, placed at the corners
of the pet's sleeping place for a week before the
move ⋆ A familiar pet toy or blanket

TIMING

The day before you move

THE SPELL

* Hold the banded agates in your open cupped hands against your navel, the sacral energy center of security for animals.

* Say, *You are always with me, even on your journey. Sleep the hours away. And I will come for you and bring you home, as soon as I may.*

* The night before the move, wrap the agates inside the blanket or next to the toy, repeating the spell words.

* Give your animal the toy/blanket and carry the agates with you, holding them to your navel regularly during the absence, to connect telepathically with the absent animal.

Moonstone Protection for Animals Who Go Out at Night

YOU WILL NEED

A moonstone or selenite crystal for each animal
★ White flower heads in water, set under each of the
three phases of the moon and then scattered

TIMING

*During the crescent or early waxing moon,
the full moon, and again during the waning moon*

THE SPELL

* Choose a night in each of the three phases of the moon and put
  your moonstone in the flower water overnight, saying as you do so,
  Daughter, Mother, Grandmother Moon, cast your light, as my [Name]
  *does roam. Light his/her way through the dangers of the night, and
  bring him/her safely home by morning light.*

* Scatter the water on the ground.

* After the waning moon, keep the moonstone by your bedside each
  night, repeating the spell words before you fall asleep.

To Protect Your Pet from Being Bullied by Other Pets or Aggressive Animals When S/he's Out and About

YOU WILL NEED

A red (preferably) or brown tiger's eye ✶ A picture of a lion/lioness with a picture of your pet underneath, faceup

TIMING

Tuesday

THE SPELL

✻ Put the tiger's eye on top of the pictures, saying, *The heart of a lion/lioness, the fierceness of the tiger's gleaming eye, any other creature will desist, As you* [name pet] *pass by.*

✻ Put your pet's picture on top of the lion's and return the tiger's eye to the top, saying, *Back off, be very afraid. My courageous pet, of strength is made. S/he will not attack if you stay away. But my* [name pet] *is a predator, don't risk being prey.*

✻ Keep the tiger's eye on top of the pictures if the bullying pet is within the home and carry the tiger's eye when you both go out.

To Protect Your Pet from Nasty Humans if the Animal Goes Out Alone or if You Suspect That Others Tease Your Pet When You are Not Looking

YOU WILL NEED

A St. Francis of Assisi medallion (obtainable online) ✴ A soft cloth ✴ Eight small, green candles, set in a square around the medallion

TIMING

Saturday during the waning moon

THE SPELL

* Polish the medallion with the cloth in alternating counterclockwise and clockwise circles, saying, *St. Francis who loved animals, keep my animal* [Name] *safe for me. From human spite and viciousness, so s/he will not be hurt or secretly caused distress.*

* Light each candle clockwise, repeating the spell words for each one and leave them to burn through.

* Put the medallion on the pet's collar, saying, *Protection is complete, none may the power of fire defeat.*

* Polish the medallion whenever you sense that your pet may be at risk, repeating the spell words.

To Calm Animals Who are Afraid of Loud Noises, Storms, Busy Streets, or Traffic

YOU WILL NEED

A recording on a smartphone or tablet of typical loud street noises or the main trigger of distress

TIMING

When the animal is not present

THE SPELL

* Gradually turn down the volume, saying as it becomes quieter, *Insulate [name animal(s)] from discordant sounds, from the sky and all around. When we go out or hear a storm, let their effects no longer resound.*

* Keep repeating the spell words and turning down the volume until there is silence.

* Play the recording to the animal on very low volume before going out.

A St. Blaise Ritual to Help Animals and Birds in Badly Run Zoos and in Circuses or Who are Overworked and/or Abused

YOU WILL NEED

A corkboard to which you have attached pictures or news items of performing abused or captive creatures from around the world, placed flat on a table ∗ An equal number of pictures of free exotic and wild creatures in their natural habitat ∗ Greenery

TIMING

When you hear of a particular atrocity

THE SPELL

∗ Pass your hands slowly, counterclockwise, palms down and horizontal, over the corkboard, saying softly, *Good St. Blaise, free from chains those creatures suffering in captivity, that they may be rescued from cruelty, to live in places of sanctuary.*

∗ Each time you finish a chant, replace a disturbing picture with one of a creature roaming free.

∗ Continue until you have replaced every picture on the corkboard.

∗ Hang the board, surrounded by greenery.

To Protect Endangered Species and Stop the Destruction of Wildlife Habitats and Pollution in the Seas

YOU WILL NEED

A small area of ground or a pot containing soil
★ A stick ★ A jug of water ★ Protective healing animal plants, such as chamomile, comfrey, echinacea, lavender, milk thistle, and sage, or indigenous greenery ★ Four moss agate crystals (optional)

TIMING

Sunday morning

THE SPELL

* Write in the soil with the stick, RESTORE GREENERY, REGROW THE TREES, MAKE LIFE THRIVE AGAIN. BRING HEALING RAIN, THE SUN THAT WARMS, AND KEEP ENDANGERED CREATURES FROM ALL HUMAN HARM.

* Pour water on the soil, saying, *Make clear the seas, that creatures may be, free to increase, not to be wiped out and cease.*

* Plant the herbs or indigenous greenery, adding, if you can get them, four moss agate crystals, saying, *All shall grow again, conservation shall not be in vain. Life and habitats shall be restored, species flourish and thrive once more.*

To Protect Animals from Poaching, Cruel Slaughterhouses, and Factory-Farming Methods That Cause Suffering

YOU WILL NEED

Twelve small, brown-colored stones
★ A pot ★ A fast-flowing stream or river

TIMING

Thursday

THE SPELL

* Build an enclosed square with the stones, naming for each one a cruelty, such as killing elephants or rhinos for their tusks.

* Then say, *Protection only words, by the guilty is unheard. Walls of profit, built of greed, animals suffering when there is no need. But walls can be knocked down indeed.*

* Remove alternating stones from the square, putting them in the pot saying, *One by one, until all bad practices shall be undone, the poachers' guns and spears be stilled, and justice for helpless creatures won.*

* Put the remaining stones in the pot, pour the pot's contents into fast-flowing water, and say, *Throughout the world, the words be heard, like water ripples spread, and cruelty finally be shed.*

To Help an Aging or Chronically Ill Pet Who Has No Energy

YOU WILL NEED

A jade crystal ✴ A bowl of water

TIMING

Early morning

THE SPELL

* Put the jade in the water bowl overnight or for three hours the day before you offer the water to the pet.

* Gently stir the water with the index finger of your dominant hand, counterclockwise, six times, saying, *Be filled with my energy, I can share and spare a little strength for you, in love from me, that each day you stronger will become and be.*

* Stir it six times clockwise, repeating the spell words.

* Take out the jade and offer the water to the pet.

To Help a Sick Animal Who Needs Veterinary Care, Yet Who Cannot Bear to Be Touched by Strangers

YOU WILL NEED

A small green bag, containing any three of the following: jade, blue calcite, rose quartz, moss agate, dried chamomile, comfrey, lavender, or sage * A printout of a picture of the vet from the internet * Three hairs from the animal

TIMING

Three days before treatment

THE SPELL

* On day 1, hold the bag, saying, *You need more help than in the home I can provide, I transfer the security you have with me to [name vet] outside. I will stay, but only skilled hands can take this pain/sickness away.*

* On day 2, add the picture of the vet to the bag, repeating the spell words.

* On day 3, add the hairs to the bag, hanging it near the front door.

* Take the bag to the appointment.

To Let a Pet Go Gently from Life

YOU WILL NEED

A quiet area where the animal will
not be disturbed ★ Water in which you have
soaked a rose quartz crystal overnight

TIMING

When you sense the pet is ready to let go

THE SPELL

* Put a drop or two of the crystal water near the pet's heart and on
  your inner wrist points for your heart center, saying, *I let you go, sadly,*
  reluctantly, but I cannot leave you in suffering and pain. You will live,
  young and free again, in my heart and memory. And one day perhaps return
  to me in actuality.

* Sit quietly by your pet, saying the spell words, softer and softer until
  they fade into silence. Repeat daily or hourly until the animal lets go
  or it is time to take the pet to the vet.

* Bury the quartz with your pet or keep it with a photo.

To Mourn the Death of a Pet

A special symbol of the pet—a collar, a medallion, or
a small pet toy ✳ Small, white, fading flowers

TIMING

The days after the cremation or burial

THE SPELL

✳ Find a place where you have happy memories with your pet and set
the symbol on the ground. Pluck fading petals from the flowers
and scatter them over it, saying, *The pain will grow less, I know,
but it is hard to let you go. To the Rainbow Bridge in heaven where
animals play. Or, if you wish, to come back to me some day.*

✳ Dig up the soft earth where the petals are scattered and the symbol
is lying, and plant a new white flowering plant there, saying,
*I do not leave your spirit behind. For wherever I go. Your essence and
love I will always find.*

✳ If you wish, scatter any ashes at the spot.

To Stop a Bird from Constantly Screeching or Feather-Ripping

YOU WILL NEED

A feather from the bird

TIMING

Every morning when you get up and every evening before you go to bed for five days

THE SPELL

* Hold the feather, facing the bird, and say nine times, each time more softly, *Softer, gentler, quieter be. Return to tranquility.*

* Keep stroking the feather, but move away from the room where the bird is, whispering the words.

* Each time you do the spell move farther away until on evening 5 you are outside the home.

* Let the feather fly away.

To Stop Your Barking or
Howling Dog or Yowling Cat

Six long hairs from the animal
* Blue thread * A thin copper bracelet

TIMING

Beginning Friday morning for six days

THE SPELL

* Attach each hair with the thread tied in six knots to the bracelet, saying, *Cease your noise, your constant howling/barking/yowling causes distress to all around. I wish to hear a softer sound. Make the volume and frequency less. Quieter be, instantly, if you wish to live with me.*

* Touch each of the hairs clockwise in turn, repeating the spell words.

* Go outdoors each morning from day 2 and cut free a hair each day until you have just the bracelet, repeating the spell words.

* Wear or hold the bracelet and continue to say the spell words each morning outside until the problem stops.

Index